I
Have
Chosen
You

A revision of the CHOICE confirmation process

in keeping with the *Catechism of the Catholic Church*

LEADER'S GUIDE

A Six-Month Confirmation Process

for Emerging Young Adults

JOSEPH MOORE

Paulist Press

New York/Mahwah, N.J.

Scripture extracts are taken from the New Revised Standard Version, Copyright © 1989, by the Division of Christian Education of the National Council of the Churches of Christ in the United States of America and reprinted by permission of the publisher.

Acknowledgments:

I would like to thank Paulist Press for permission to reprint material from two of my earlier works, *Fastened on God* and *Prayers for a New Generation*, published by Paulist Press.

To Alfred A. Knopf, Inc. for permission to copy pages 17–18 in *The Prophet* by Kahlil Gibran (New York, 1982).

Permission is granted by Paulist Press to the reader to copy for educational use those pages so designated, in particular the sponsor and retreat materials, the Rite of Choice, the Rite of Enrollment, the Penance Service, the "Waiting Prayer Service," and the test in Session 11. None of these materials are in the **Journal** for *I Have Chosen You.*

Cover and book design by Lynn Else

ISBN: 0-8091-9578-X

Published by Paulist Press
997 Macarthur Boulevard
Mahwah, New Jersey 07430

www.paulistpress.com

Printed and bound in the
United States of America

Contents

INTRODUCTION

The Theology of the Sacrament of Confirmation: A Synopsis

Confirmation is one of the "sacraments of Christian initiation" along with baptism and the Eucharist. Confirmation completes the grace we receive at baptism. Through it we are more united to the church and are given a special strength from the Holy Spirit to be witnesses of Jesus Christ. In the Roman Catholic Church, the tradition is to wait until a child is able to reason before this sacrament is administered. Ordinarily a bishop celebrates confirmation in order to signify the deepening of the union between the candidate and the church.

Confirmation is sometimes called the "sacrament of Christian maturity." It is important to realize that the grace of baptism is a free gift and does not need "ratification" to become effective. To put it another way, we do not "earn" this sacrament. In the United States, there is the widespread custom of receiving confirmation somewhere between the ages of twelve and eighteen (although some dioceses and parishes have restored the practice of receiving this sacrament along with the Eucharist).To this end, parishes all over the country have developed programs of preparation for preteens and teenagers. The purpose of these programs, along with *I Have Chosen You,* is to help young people to spiritually prepare to belong more fully to Jesus Christ and his church. We have selected this program's title, designed primarily for high school age adolescents, from Jesus' words to his disciples in the Gospel according to John.

> **You did not choose me but I chose you. And I anointed you to go and bear fruit, fruit that will last, so that the Father will give you whatever you ask him in my name. I am giving you these commands so that you may love one another.**
>
> **(John 15:16–17)**

Because in the United States we are often dealing with adolescents as the parish community's confirmation candidates, our programs are quite structured and contain guidelines for this preparation process. This is because both younger and older adolescents function best when demands upon them are clear, consistent, and defined. But this has to do with adolescence and not with the nature of confirmation. Since the sacraments are a free gift of God, no "obstacle course," no adherence to some catechetical program, allows a person to "achieve" reception of this sacrament. A danger exists that this mistaken notion might be conveyed to young people by well-meaning catechists. We must constantly work with the tension between the value of structured confirmation programs and a theological understanding of God's total graciousness to us despite our unworthiness. The sacramental preparation process of *I Have Chosen You* is to help young people "accept for themselves the faith in which they have been baptized" (Rite of Baptism for Children, No. 3).

Philosophy of *I Have Chosen You*

The philosophical underpinnings of this sacramental preparation process are documents of the church, and in particular the *Catechism of the Catholic Church,* as well as the *General Catechetical Directory* and *Renewing the Vision.*

The *Catechism of the Catholic Church*, published in 1994, is a reference text of catechesis for the entire church. It is a compilation of Catholic doctrine illuminated by scripture, tradition, and the teaching authority of the church. It is a source for people of faith to deepen their knowledge of Jesus Christ. **(We strongly suggest that as a catechist you obtain a copy of this catechism to assist you in your preparation of each session.)**

The *General Catechetical Directory* (published by the United States Catholic Conference of Bishops, 1998), which is also a guideline for the entire church, states that "the aim of catechesis is to bring people into mature communion with Jesus Christ through the community of faith" (GCD 80, 82). This simple statement sums up the whole sacramental preparation process of *I Have Chosen You*. This document reminds us that "faith is to be believed, celebrated, lived and prayed"(GCD 122). The fundamental tasks of catechesis include promoting the knowledge of faith, liturgical education, moral formation, how to pray, and how to be a community as well as witnesses to the gospel (GCD 85–86). "Catechesis shapes the minds, hearts, and spirit of believers, forming them as disciples" (GCD 87).

Renewing the Vision: A Framework for Catholic Youth Ministry (published by the U.S.C.C., 1997)

I Have Chosen You has attempted to incorporate the goals of ministry with youth as outlined in this document

- to empower young people to live as disciples of Jesus Christ in our world today (RTV, p. 9)

- to draw young people to responsible participation in the life, mission, and work of the Catholic faith community (RTV, p. 11)

- to foster the total personal and spiritual growth of each young person (RTV, p. 15)

R.C.I.A.: Model of the Preparation for Confirmation in *I Have Chosen You*

Catechesis is an education in the faith of children, young people and adults which includes especially the teaching of Christian doctrine imparted, generally speaking, in an organic and systematic way, with a view to initiating the hearers into the fullness of the Christian life. (*Catechism of the Catholic Church, No. 5*)

The first point we need to make is that this book is much more of a "process" than a "program." A program connotes a well-defined collection of material or lessons, which, if the person passes, entitles him or her to receive some type of certificate, entitlement, or graduation. A process, on the other hand, recognizes the fact that we are dealing with varying levels of maturity and that everyone is not at the same level—in this case not at the same level of faith formation. It recognizes that some young people are in need of more evangelization, learning about Jesus and the message of the gospel. Sadly, in our church today we have many baptized, unevangelized teenagers.

I Have Chosen You is modeled, in terms of its format, on a document entitled "The Rite of Christian Initiation of Adults" (R.C.I.A.). This document outlines a parish community approach to the incorporation of converts into the Catholic Church. It is a process of initiation rooted in the liturgical life of the church. It emphasizes the key role of the individual's sponsor in the faith. Because of the richness of this process, and because confirmation is one of the sacraments of initiation, we have used it as a model to follow in **I Have Chosen You**. Our book is also rooted in the National Catechetical Directory's "Sharing the Light of Faith" (U.S.C.C., 1979) that maintains the entire parish community should be involved in the catechesis of its members. Catechesis is not restricted to learning doctrine; it also involves individual and liturgical prayer, Christian service, ministry, and the experience of a faith community—themes which are echoed in the General Catechetical Directory.

This sacramental preparation process is a mirror of the R.C.I.A. and is divided into four distinct periods:

Precatechumenate: A time when the candidate is evangelized, and learns about Jesus and the good news

Catechumenate: A period of intense Christian formation

Purification and Enlightenment: During Lent, the proximate preparation for initiation into the faith

Mystagogia: Meaning "instruction in the mysteries"; after the newly baptized are fully initiated into the sacramental life of the church, they are instructed in a more specific way about the faith.

To reflect the R.C.I.A. in our own process of preparation for confirmation, we divide the twenty-four sessions in the following manner.

Sacramental Preparation Process

Precatechumenate

Introductory session (1)
"Twilight" Retreat (2)
Sessions 3–7
Individual interviews

Catechumenate

Rite of Choice
Sessions 8–11
Examination
Community Service Project (12)
Parent/Candidate "Mini" Retreat (13)
Sessions 14–17

Period of Purification and Enlightenment

Rite of Enrollment
Sponsor/Candidate "Mini" Retreat (18)
Sessions 19–22
Retreat weekend (23)
Penance Service
Confirmation Rehearsal/"Waiting" prayer service (24)

(preparation process continues on next page)

Parish Celebration of the Sacrament of Confirmation

Period of Mystagogy

The ongoing involvement of the confirmed in the liturgical and prayer life of the parish, in service, in youth ministry, and ongoing religious education

A Process Outline

I Have Chosen You is ordinarily designed to be completed in twenty-four sessions (including the retreats) and two rites during the liturgy, plus a penance service. It fits well into one academic year if meetings are weekly. If meetings are monthly, then it is a process which can be spread over two academic years or calendar years. Do not forget that sessions may need to be postponed due to inclement weather, school vacations, and conflicts with school and parish events.

The Role of the Sponsor

To emphasize the unity between the sacraments of baptism and confirmation, it is desirable that one of the baptismal sponsors be chosen. If this is not feasible or possible, we again look to the R.C.I.A. model. Sponsors should not be chosen to flatter a relative or simply because the person is admired by the teenager. A sponsor for confirmation should be:

1. a practicing, faith-filled Roman Catholic adult or young adult already fully initiated into the faith himself or herself, who has no canonical impediments;

2. able to form a relationship with a young person;

3. willing to give the time to participate in the sacramental preparation process and to pray for the candidate;

4. willing to share his or her own experience of faith.

The sponsor may not be a parent of the candidate. For this reason, we clearly distinguish between the parental and sponsor components of *I Have Chosen You.* As members of the faith community, and because of their own special relationship with their son or daughter, parents ought not to be mere bystanders to the confirmation preparation process. It is desirable that the candidate choose a sponsor early in the preparation process and invite that person to attend the "Rite of Choice." The young person ought to take great care in choosing his or her sponsor to be a "friend for the journey."

The "Sharing Group": Locus of Adolescent Religious Education

I Have Chosen You has as its mainstay the weekly sharing group. It is our thesis that it is the small sharing group of people of any age that is the "place" for religious education. In the past we have borrowed from the classroom model in structuring our religious education; we suggest here that it is more appropriate to borrow from the group model. The Second Vatican Council described the principal aims of Christian education to be: "...that as the baptized person is gradually introduced into a knowledge of the mystery of salvation, he may daily grow more conscious of the gift of faith which he has received; that he may learn to adore God the Father in spirit and in truth...that he may be trained to conduct his personal life in righteousness and in the sanctity of truth...." (Declaration on Christian Education, n. 2). In their pastoral letter, "To Teach as Jesus Did," the United States Catholic bishops also focused on community when they wrote: "The education mission of the Church is an integrated ministry embracing three interlocking dimensions: the message revealed by God which the Church proclaims, fellowship in the life of the Holy Spirit, and service to the Christian community and the entire human community" ("To Teach as Jesus Did," U.S.C.C., 1973, n. 14).

Again, with regard to its educational mission, youth leaders engaged in religious education need to ask: Where can God's message best be proclaimed? Where can this fellowship spilling over into service best be experienced? We submit that the small sharing group is preferential to the classroom in the fulfillment of these purposes.

In another document, published by the department of education of the U.S.C.C., "A Vision of Youth Ministry" (1976), it states: "In the life of a community, young people and a few significant adults learn to listen to one another, and, in doing so, to hear God speak. As they try to help each other express in words the truth they experience, they learn a living theology. In this kind of community youth have a mutual ministry to each other. They share themselves, their convictions, their faith with each other" (p. 8).

Group work had its origins in the creativity of J. Pratt who, in 1905, began didactic and inspirational group meetings to encourage the morale of physically ill patients whose activities were restricted (e.g., tubercular).

The support group, even for adults, functions unconsciously as a family with the leader representing the parent role. Through the support offered by peers and the leader, individuals learn to reveal themselves and experience both acceptance (leading to self-acceptance) and the objective viewpoints of others. Inner strength is often enhanced through sharing with others, as is the ability to cope with common problems. In these groups, the leader assumes a passive role with the group itself structuring its own leadership. A more appropriate term for leader here is *facilitator.* Through the sharing of a common "plight," support group members often experience a reduction of stress, renewed energy, and an improved self-esteem. Support groups resemble real-life and ordinary human interaction, thus gracing the process with continuous doses of reality for the participant. There is much literature today in the area of group dynamics and we would recommend some reading for anyone engaged in the formal religious education of youth.

Implications for Religious Education

It is not our intent to declare that all religious education is to abandon the classroom model and follow the support group model. Rather, it is our suggestion that the group models a more appropriate context than does the traditional classroom for the experience of growing in faith, and we say this for a variety of reasons. First of all, the environment teaches as much as the lesson. A classroom is formal where people are separated from each other in separate desks. A group environment is informal where people sit facing each other in chairs or perhaps even, for youth, on the floor. An equation of warmth and informality, where a person is free to be himself or herself, and where life and faith experience is easily shared is most desirable. A group meeting in a home-like atmosphere (not necessarily in a home per se, however) is definitely sending a different message than the functionality of a traditional classroom. Also, size contributes to environment. Group sizes ideally are eight to twelve members, whereas classrooms can accommodate as many people as there are desks.

The leader in a group or facilitator exercises a much lower-key role than the traditional teacher. The leader physically sits on the same level as the participants and has as his or her role the function of keeping the group focused and from time to time being didactic when his or her expertise, life experience, or knowledge of the Catholic faith is needed. We would submit that this role of facilitator is more appropriate to the religious educator of youth than is the authoritarian role of the teacher in the classroom.

Community, an atmosphere of openness and trust, is much more attainable in a small sharing group than in a class. Appropriate sharing of faith as well as the mutual struggles of life can more easily occur within this context. Through this sharing and the ensuing group support, a young person can grow both in self-esteem and in the understanding that his or her religion is rooted in authentic community. Personal values and a deeper grasp of one's personal faith are nourished in such an atmosphere. Also, of course, instruction can still occur within the group but the demands of the context itself insure the connectedness of what is taught to real life. John Shea, who writes so articulately about the sharing of our personal stories in the light of the gospel story, has remarked that it takes life experience to render the gospel credible (National Symposium on Catholic Youth Ministry, October 1983, New York). Very often we make a mistake in preaching and teaching by dwelling on the meaning of a New Testament text at length and barely touching upon our life experience. What we need to do more is to share, explore our common life experiences in depth, and then to turn to the gospel for deeper meaning. But what we often do in education is to give our collective experience short shrift. We don't talk it out together, plumb its depths by discussing it within the context of a trusting community which is where the Spirit can be revealed—through each other. For example, it might be a teacher's temptation to elaborate on the gospel story of Jesus calming the storm without first having invited students to share at length the "storms" of their own existence, and in which areas of their lives they need to deepen trust in God. In other words, the gospel story needs to be personalized for each of us in the sharing of our own stories.

Translating the Sharing Group into Christian Community

Let us look at the work of a prominent religious educator in the United States and then reflect upon the words of two theologians. John Westerhoff, in his book *Will Our Children Have Faith?* maintains that faith is not passed from generation to generation through schooling, but rather through a faith-filled community. (Westerhoff, John, *Will Our Children Have Faith?* New York: Seabury Press, 1972, p. 80). He talks about enculturation as opposed to indoctrination. It is the faithful congregation or parish community that through its very life and vitality transmits the faith to young people. In this sense, every member of the faith community, not just the priests or youth minister or director of religious education, has a responsibility to minister with young people and to absorb them into the adult community of faith. *Koinonia* is the New Testament Greek word for ministry as togetherness, fellowship, participation, and communion with one another.

Catholic theologian, Thomas Groome, wrote the following:

> ...all people should find their local parish a truly "Catholic" community, a place of welcome and inclusion, where all can feel a sense of belonging and being "at home." It is to be a place of service and empowerment to service, where peoples' needs are met and their gifts employed. Faith develop-

ment researchers say that young people have even a greater felt need for a sense of "belonging" to their parish than do adults; they also warn that many congregations fail particularly in this regard. Interviews with young people who have "left the church" often reveal that many don't feel they have left, but that they never belonged. (Groome, Thomas, "Parish as Catechist," *Church,* Fall 1990, Vol. 6, No. 3, p 25)

These reflections tell us that it is not only the small sharing group in which confirmation candidates participate that needs to provide an experience of community. These young people also need to experience the same type of welcome and sense of belonging in the parish community as a whole. Otherwise, the confirmation process is a satellite experience unrelated to the life of the entire faith community.

Last, let us look at some reflections on community by the Lutheran theologian, Dietrich Bonhoeffer, who was imprisoned by the Nazis in World War II and eventually murdered by them. His most influential book is called *The Cost of Discipleship.* Bonhoeffer reminds us of truths we should not lose sight of as we attempt to build a sharing group model for our adolescent catechesis. True community cannot be manufactured by human effort alone, but it is created in and through Jesus Christ. The experience of true community is then a gift and is the setting for ministry with one another. It is through the power of Christ that each of us can set aside our self-centeredness and enter into and become committed to a community beyond ourselves. (Bonhoeffer, Dietrich, *Life Together,* New York: Harper and Row, 1954). These words of Bonhoeffer are echoed in the *Catechism of the Catholic Church* in its section on "Communion." There we are reminded of the scriptures: "If one member suffers, all suffer together; if one member is honored, all rejoice together. Now you are the body of Christ and individually members of it" (CCC, No. 953).

Suggestions for Group Facilitators/Catechists

To assist you in the formation of your sharing group we will offer ten suggestions—the "Ten Commandments" for group facilitators. We would like to caution that the group approach in no way minimizes the leader's responsibility to direct the group and not to tolerate any disruptive, rude, or inappropriate behavior. The leader should also try to recognize the young person for whom being in the group is difficult—due to shyness, defensiveness, or lack of similar communication at home. (For many young people today the group becomes a surrogate family because of the severe absence of such in their lives.) The leader can call upon his or her living skills to recognize and handle fundamental defense mechanisms which inhibit group process, such as intellectualizing, projecting, and dominating the conversation. Be ready to respond helpfully if strong feelings (e.g., sorrow, anger) noticeably well up in a young person. Keep the group focused on its purposes and do not allow it to stray into an undirected rap session.

In *The Wounded Healer* (New York: Image Books, 1979, p. 94) Henri Nouwen wrote: "A Christian community is therefore a healing community not because wounds are cured and pains are alleviated, but because wounds and pains become openings or occasions for a new vision. Mutual confession then becomes a mutual deepening of hope, and sharing weakness becomes a reminder to one and all of the coming strength."

"TEN COMMANDMENTS" FOR A GROUP LEADER

1. Remind the group about confidentiality. The group should be a safe place to speak.

2. Have the group sit physically close so that all can see each other; no one should be on the perimeter.

3. Eye contact: Fix your gaze upon the person who is speaking. Persons may need the strength of your eyes to allow them to speak. Also be sure the group members can all see each other easily.

4. Don't give advice all of the time. People, even teenagers, need to solve their own problems. Don't fall into this easy trap out of your own need to rescue others from life's difficult moments.

5. Listen! It is by being listened to attentively that we discover our solutions which lie buried within us.

6. Silence—don't be afraid of it. Allow it to exist. It has a creativity and pressure of its own far superior to any pressure you may exert to get the group to speak.

7. Your own story of faith is significant to the group, but remember that you are there for others. If you wish to identify with the speaker, do so in a very simple statement: for example, "I know what you mean because my father also tended to drink too much." There will be occasions to share the wisdom of your own experience. Talking about yourself frequently, however, is not proper to your role.

8. Non-verbal clues: Focus more on the feelings of the speaker than on his or her words. Words are often a protective screen to what is really going on inside. *But remember at all times that your role is not that of a therapist or counselor. If you observe emotional problems, refer that young person to someone who can help, a trained therapist or school counselor.*

9. Keep the group discussion focused on one person's issues at a time. Don't let some group member manipulate you to turn the spotlight on him or her while somebody still has unfinished business. Never leave a person out there "hanging." Ideally all group members should respond to each person. At a very minimum the leader must respond. Encourage the responses of others.

10. Tone: By sharing your own life experience and faith journey, you provide the young people with a model of what is appropriate for discussion within the group. You set the tone.

Do not be put off by these suggestions if you do not automatically possess all these skills. These are ideals toward which a group leader strives, and most of us learn them in the doing. Also, don't forget that the Holy Spirit is at work in the hearts of these young people and is the primary "teacher" and facilitator of growth. So relax, be yourself, and do your best.

More on Qualifications of the Catechist

A minister is not a doctor whose primary task is to take away pain. Rather, he deepens the pain to a level where it can be shared...creates a unity based on the shared confession of our basic brokenness and on a shared hope. This hope in turn leads us far beyond the boundaries of human togetherness to Him who calls His people away from the land of slavery to the land of freedom. (Henri Nouwen, *The Wounded Healer,* New York; Doubleday Image, 1979)

Do not say that you are not qualified to work with **I Have Chosen You** because you are not formally trained in religious education nor a theologian. Studies show that academic background does not determine a successful catechist. One study found that two of the three determinants for success in youth ministry groups are (a) a feeling of being among peer friends (i.e., a sense of the group as a community), and (b) the quality of their personal relationship with the adult leader. Also the work of Merton Strommen on people who are successful in ministry indicates that the two ingredients which count most, more than skills and academic knowledge, are (a) an open, warm, and affirming attitude, and (b) a lively faith in the minister. So as a leader of youth, your qualifications do not lie primarily in the academic realm. Of course, you are an adult, and this research implies a good adult-youth interpersonal relationship. It does not say that adults should act as peers of teenagers. It does say that adults should act as caring persons.

Structure of the Weekly Session

The suggested time frame:

Unless otherwise noted, we would recommend that sessions last seventy-five minutes in order to allow enough time for prayer, music, and an occasional audio-visual or guest speaker. It is important to get the group used to the fact that you start on time. It is considerate to those who are coming to pick up the young people to end on time with each session.

1. **Preparation. *The Catechetical Leader's Guide*** contains reflections on each topic of each session which involves the discussion group. The reflection begins with a short reference to the *Catechism of the Catholic Church*. What follows is not theological writing, but rather ideas for presentation or discussion of the material. These reflections are based in sound Catholic thinking and represent years of my experience in religious education and catechesis with young people. Hopefully these insights will provide you with food for thought, both for yourself and for the group, and hopefully as well you will be able to draw on them to generate discussion. It is also important as a catechist that you do reading of your own, and review the topics in this book by turning to Catholic publications, as well as helpful Catholic resource sites on the Internet. Conversations with other faith-filled adults, and brainstorming with other catechists, can also provide you with insights to be shared with your group.

2. **Opening**. Since it is important for the group members to unwind from their busy lives, it is important to spend at least five minutes establishing a spiritual mood at the start of each session. Therefore, it is advised to light a candle if permitted and to listen to a recorded song related to the theme of the session (either a religious song or one indirectly related by its faith message). The

quality of the sound system should be good—don't forget that "the medium is the message." One approach would be to assign group members to choose/bring a tape or CD the following week according to the pre-announced theme. Or perhaps you would invite them to do so whenever someone expresses a wish for it. (Their choices might be more contemporary and more meaningful to them than yours may be, but you would need to screen the lyrics before the song is played.) After the song, allow a few moments of quiet and begin with an opening prayer read either by you or by one of the group members. **Many sessions provide an opening prayer. You may also create your own prayer, or have spontaneous prayer with your group.**

3. **Materials**. Each teenager should bring his or her journal every week in which are located exercises to be completed and shared. You as the group leader will need a journal as well. Also they will have to bring a pen or you will need to provide pens. **(For sessions 3–7, 16, 19, and 20 you will also need to bring a New Testament.)** The text to be discussed for each session is included for you in this book. You may want to ask group members to bring a New Testament every week, if you feel it helpful to do so. **(You will need the Old Testament for Session 22.)**

4. **The Exercises or Group Activities**. Some sessions require more "teaching"—particularly the ones pertaining to doctrine. The majority of sessions, however, are designed for learning through group sharing. Toward this end two exercises are provided to stimulate conversation. The exercise is not an end in itself—it is merely a springboard for discussion that hopefully will lead to a deepening of faith. Our experience is that it is much easier with teenagers to generate a discussion to give them a chance to think and write their reflections on paper first. This helps the discussion to remain focused and gives the youth the security of a piece of paper from which to share. To simplify matters, the exercises appear only in the journal, not in your Catechist Guide. The directions are clearly given with each one. In most cases written responses are requested that are then shared with the group. As you prepare each week for the upcoming session, be sure to peruse each appropriate exercise in your journal. Don't be afraid to augment an exercise or tailor it more personally to your group. Trust your own ingenuity. Most people learn best when they are actively involved in the learning process. This is especially true of teenagers who are sorting out their values and shaping their identities.

I Have Chosen You is designed to involve young people in learning through the discussion of various topics of significance to their lives and to faith. To be a catalyst to this process is the role of the group leader or catechist. To be effective in this area is a real challenge. It would be much easier to use a textbook where the young people take turns reading aloud. But research tells us that very little learning or personal growth occurs in this way. Part of the challenge of the leader is to develop the skills we discussed in the introduction, those of facilitating a group as the "leading-learner." (One clever way to state the leader's role is to see oneself more as a "guide on the side" than a "sage on the stage.") These skills can take time to develop, and patience with oneself is required. It is important not to give in to feelings of self-defeat when a session goes poorly or when a particular group is difficult to engage in discussion. It is a gradual process to learn to become comfortable with silences, to draw out reticent participants, and to provoke a lively discussion. There is really no way to learn how to lead a group better than to do it. By trial and error, and by exploring various options, an individual grows and becomes seasoned in the art of facilitating and faith-sharing.

In your **Catechetical Leader's Guide** there are two discussion questions in each learning session designed to provide the leader with additional discussion material. Each group has a particular and unique complexion; no two groups are alike. Some groups are extremely verbal, and with them just one question may stimulate forty-five minutes of discussion. Others may be composed of less mature individuals, or more inhibited personalities, and these may require more material to stimulate interaction. These discussion questions were designed for such groups especially. Don't be afraid of adding your own discussion questions either as you ponder the topic during your preparation period.

5. **Audio-Visuals**. Audio-visuals are not "addenda" to learning experiences; they are an integral part of them. Try to preview any A-V you intend to use to decide where in the session you wish to present it. You may wish to check your local library for possible free loan videos/films. Diocesan offices also often give out films and videos at a nominal rental free. Another suggestion is to ask teens to pick out slides, perhaps 12–20, and set them to a particular song which expresses the theme of an upcoming session. Another approach is to show short, relevant clips from current movies in VHS or DVD format.

6. **Closure.** It is important to start and end each session in prayer. Spontaneous prayer is an excellent form, and/or members could take turns leading prayer or sharing a reading. It is important that both you and the group members are comfortable with whatever form your prayer takes—but this relaxation in group prayer may take time to develop. So be patient with the process. Another recorded song is also an appropriate way to end the session. You can either repeat the song you used to open the session, or choose something else, or let the teenager bring in a song suitable to the theme. (Again, it is advisable to listen to the lyrics of the song beforehand and to ensure that the music itself is conducive to a prayerful mood.) We would suggest that the final ten minutes (including the selected song) be devoted to prayer.

Suggestions for the format of a closing prayer are to be found in the following sessions:

Session 4	See **Journal**
Session 5	See **Journal**
Session 9	See **Catechetical Leader's Guide**
Session 10	See **Journal**
Session 11	See **Journal**
(Session 15	To end the session, a special suggestion to share food as a group)
Session 19	See **Catechetical Leader's Guide**
Session 21	See **Journal**
Session 22	See **Journal**

7. **Homework**. There is only one test which requires any home study.

A Final Note. This sacramental preparation process is based in large part on group sharing as we have already discussed. Young people are often hesitant to share verbally because of the insecurity of being an adolescent. Yet we know from sound psychology that it is precisely in this act of verbally sharing who I am (or think I am) and the struggles I am undergoing that I discover my identity. This search for identity is considered by most prominent psychologists (such as Erik Erikson) to be the primary task of the teenager. So by encouraging them to share their thoughts and feelings aloud we are doing young people a beautiful service, a genuine ministry. However—and this is simply a caution—if a youth in your group is extremely unwilling to share verbally with the group, he or she ought not to be forced into sharing. This reticence could be the by-product of some emotional scars and to chastise or threaten a youth who wishes to remain silent could be somewhat traumatic and contribute to negative feelings about confirmation preparation. This young person may need simply to listen to the sharing of others and to benefit in that way only. If this silence is chronic you will want to talk about this with him or her individually, and perhaps consult with the parish youth minister, director of religious education, or priest. In any event, the rule of thumb is to always allow someone who does not wish to speak in a group to pass, and never to force that person to share his or her thoughts and feelings.

Session Preparation Plan for Each Meeting with Your Group

1. Read the background material in this Catechist's Guide for the session.

2. Decide if an audio-visual will be used, and if so, decide at which point in the session.

3. Read over the discussion questions.

4. Turn to the Journal and review the exercises for the session.

5. Choose a recorded song and reading, or a prayer (if you do not opt for the suggested opening prayer) for the session (unless these have already been assigned).

6. Decide how you will present the topic(s) of the session. You may simply wish to use an exercise to start conversation on the topic, or you may have another approach of your own to introduce what the session is about. Either way is acceptable.

7. Be sure you have gathered or ordered the materials you will need for the session.

8. Plan the manner in which you will bring closure to the session: another recorded song, a scripture reading, a shared prayer experience, and so on, or the suggestion in your Catechist's Guide or in the Journal.

9. Never leave this preparation for the last minute just before the session—you will not be properly prepared.

10. Note that some sessions suggest an invited guest/speaker. Be sure to arrange for this well in advance.

   Session 1: Your pastor (this, of course, does not mean that the parish priests should be limited to one visit) A young adult, preferably from the parish, already confirmed

   Session 2: Two teenagers or young adults, preferably from the parish, already confirmed
   Another catechist or adult to assist you with supervision (or more than one for a large group)

Session 10: A parish priest or professional religious educator (i.e., someone with a background in theology)

Session 13: A teenager or young adult, already confirmed, preferably from the parish
The parent of a teenager or young adult, already confirmed, preferably from the parish

Session 18: A confirmed young adult, preferably from the parish
A member of the parish staff who is able to discuss the role of the sponsor

Session 20: A Religious Sister or Brother, or a seminarian, or a Catholic lay volunteer in a formal program

Session 23: A retreat team composed of older teens and/or young adults, and adults: one per small group
A priest to celebrate the Eucharist; other adults if needed as chaperones

Introductory Parent Session
(60 Minutes)

We suggest that as you begin this sacramental preparation process in your parish, you meet with the parents of the confirmation candidates.

A. Be sure each person receives a name tag.

B. After welcoming the parents recite an opening prayer (one suggestion: a verse of the hymn "Come, Holy Ghost").

C. Divide parents into small groups (if there is more than just your group) with the adults who will be working with their teenagers. Have each parent complete the sentence (those who are confirmed Catholics): "The thing I remember about my own confirmation..." (This exercise should last 10–15 minutes; it will help people to relax, meet each other, and set the stage for section D.) If they are not confirmed Catholics, ask them for a childhood recollection of going to church, or of religion in general.

D. Discuss the introductory material on confirmation and the R.C.I.A. to be reflected in *I Have Chosen You*. Emphasize the parental support, example, and encouragement that adolescents need. (15 minutes)

E. Allow for questions/exchange. (10 minutes)

F. Review practical details.

G. A closing prayer by the pastor (the pastor's presence lends support to the sacramental preparation process). Remind them of the closing parent/youth retreat day after session twelve. **Give the date to them now so that they can reserve it**.

While parent permission forms are not legal documents, they do testify to the prudence and good judgment of the confirmation director. It is our suggestion that you ask parents to sign permission forms regarding the participation of their children in the site service projects, the weekend retreat, and even any other "off-church-property." A sample form appears below.

I give permission for my son/daughter(N)_____, to attend the (service project, retreat, etc.)_____ at (designate site) _____ on (date)_____. I understand that the mode of transportation to this event will be _____ for which I also give my permission.

In the event of a medical emergency, I give permission for the program director to obtain the services of a licensed physician. I would also like to make you aware of the following special medical condition of my son/daughter (if applies/also include permission for medication needed outside of an emergency situation). In the event of an emergency please call

_____ at # _____

Signed (Parent or Guardian)_____

Date_____

PRECATECHUMENATE

We have today in the North American Church many teenagers presenting themselves for confirmation, almost all of whom have been baptized as infants. While statistical evidence is difficult to come by, it is a fact that many of these young people "come out of the woodwork" in parishes because their parents feel they are responsible to see that their son or daughter receives this sacrament. In some of these families there is no practice of the faith. In others of these families one wonders if the teens attend church because they actually have responded to the call of the gospel. In still other families the faith is quite alive and has been nourished and developed in the lives of all the members.

As a catechist or group leader you will probably have all three of these types of young people in your group. Technically, the precatechumenate phase refers to the period prior to the catechumenate which prepares the candidate for the sacraments of initiation. It is called a time of "evangelization" where the individual becomes acquainted with the Christian community and the basic messages of Jesus. It is our feeling that we need to provide our youth with an evangelization period because of the aforementioned situation that is partially resultant from infant baptism. We call this the "precatechumenate in italics" because again, technically, it is inappropriate to baptized Christians. So for the first seven sessions the young people are asked to come together to begin to experience some measure of community, to reflect on the fact of their baptism, and examine the basics of a Christian lifestyle as found in the gospel.

Individual interviews: At the conclusion of these seven sessions we suggest that either the pastor or his delegate, or you as the group leader, have a brief conversation with each confirmation candidate. Some suggested questions for this interview are:

1. Do you feel you have some grasp of Jesus' message?

2. Do you feel you experience God in your life? How?

3. What value do you see in receiving the sacrament of confirmation?

4. Are there any basic questions that you have?

Seeing each young person individually is strongly recommended as a way to contribute to his or her own sense of self-worth and to highlight his or her individual significance to the community. It also helps the candidates to focus more clearly on their choice to be a part of the confirmation process. Last, it provides the opportunity for clarification of individual issues and questions. These interviews culminate in a Sunday liturgy which includes the "Rite of Choice."

SESSION 1: Introductory Session

Since this is the first day or night of the program, "public relations" is a key issue. The young people are probably present at the insistence of their parents or parish priest. Even though they may actually enjoy gathering with their friends, they may not be too willing to display that fact lest they be viewed as "too religious" by their peers. So if you sense any reticence or resistance, don't take it personally—it's par for the course.

FIRST QUARTER HOUR

Welcome everyone and identify yourself. Tell them you hope to give them an overview of *I Have Chosen You*. Explain the philosophy of the program as outlined in this book. Make it very clear that while there is no such thing as being forced into receiving a sacrament, some basis is needed upon which to make a judgment. Explain that that is why you, their parents, and the parish staff want very much for them to participate in this process—so that they can make a free and enlightened decision about following Jesus Christ as a young adult. Stress that attendance will be very important each week as a matter of justice to the community which is their group. Without making threats, state very simply that rude and disruptive behavior will not be tolerated, and that any display of such will indicate to you that the individual does not have the maturity required to participate in the process. (Don't feel that mention of this topic will put a damper on the group; it is crucial to establish yourself right from the outset as the person in charge.) If you are requiring that a New Testament be brought for sessions three to seven, mention it.

SECOND QUARTER HOUR

There should be a presentation by an older teenager or young adult. It is most helpful in the very first session to employ peer ministry and to have a young person who has already been confirmed talk with your group about his or her own religious experience. Obviously you want to ask a young person of faith for whom Jesus Christ is an important part of his or her life. The witness value of this talk will be something you will never be able to measure. (It's important that you discuss the *I Have Chosen You* process with the speaker beforehand so that what he or she has to say is consistent with your own goals.)

SECOND HALF HOUR

Complete and discuss as a group the "Initial Questionnaire" in the Journal.

CONCLUSION

If the "Initial Questionnaire" has elicited some negativity regarding past religious education, end on a positive note, encouraging your young people to accept the challenge of this sacramental preparation process. Remind them that the more of themselves they put into the sessions, the more meaningful will their experience be. Remind them also that building a Christian community requires the willingness of everyone who is a member of the group. It won't just "happen."

Assign them to bring a photo next week for the "Twilight" Retreat. It should be a photo of themselves as a baby. If such a photo is not available, then one as a small child will suffice. (It is so important for everyone to have a photo that you may decide to request it for this introductory session, lest someone forget it at the next session.) Pass out any important schedules or lists of dates they should keep in mind. Advance notice always minimizes potential conflicts.

Explain the Journal. For the confirmation preparation all candidates will complete a journal. Included in it are exercises for all sessions and retreat materials. Advise them not to read ahead because much of the material only makes sense in the context in which it is completed. Announce whether or not journals will be kept by the catechist or brought each week by the candidates.

End the session with a simple prayer. You might wish to light a candle, put it in the center of the group, and dim the lights in order to emphasize the specialness of this time. If you are comfortable with spontaneous prayer, you could ask the Lord to bless this group and to unite its members to each other as well as to himself as the year progresses. Or you may prefer to simply say the Lord's Prayer. Whatever you do, establish right from the start that each session will end in a prayerful way and will be a special few moments for the group.

SESSION 2: "Twilight" Retreat

Time: 3 1/2 hours (suggested time frame is 5:00 P.M.–8:30 P.M. with supper from 6:20 P.M.–6:45 P.M.)

Theme: Baptism

Materials needed: pencils, glue, candle, crucifix

5:00 P.M.

Welcome by the Leader. (This session should be held in a comfortable environment—ideally a large carpeted room with soft lighting. The group could simply sit on the floor.) The leader explains to the group(s) that the theme for the evening is baptism, a sacrament we all have received. But most of us cannot recall the event since we receive it at infancy. It's a gift from God we take for granted, as we do one of its effects: membership in the Christian community. The outset of this twilight retreat gives the leader a catechetical moment to give a brief instruction on the sacrament. A suggested outline follows:

Instruction:

Baptism is a sacrament, which means a special encounter with Jesus Christ at a special moment of our personal history.

Baptism is the first step in what we call "Christian Initiation." It is the beginning of the Christian life for a person, which is the reason parents are encouraged to bring children for baptism soon after birth—so that the Christian life can begin as soon as possible.

"Holy Baptism is the basis of the whole Christian life...through baptism we are freed from sin and reborn as sons of God; we become members of the Church and are made sharers in her mission" (CCC #1213).

"In the very early Christian Church it was the baptismal act with which the convert began to 'live a new life.' It symbolized a fundamental inner change from no belief to believing that Jesus Christ is God and that we are united in a bond with him to the Father. 'Baptism is birth into new life in Christ'" (CCC #1277).

Jesus answered, **"Very truly I tell you, no one can enter the kingdom of God without being born of water and Spirit"** (John 3:5). By our baptism we are freed from our human destiny of sin and separation from God (called "original sin") and drawn into the community of faith and love.

"In the early Church, the manner of receiving this sacrament was a total immersion in water as the words of Baptism were pronounced. This was to demonstrate new life. (*Baptism* comes from a Greek word meaning to plunge or immerse.) Today we symbolize immersion by pouring water over the person's head. A priest is the normal minister of Baptism—but in an emergency any Christian can baptize. 'For all the baptized children or adults, faith must grow after Baptism'" (CCC #1254).

Tell the group that the basic understanding of Christian baptism is outlined at the end of Session One in their Journals. After your short presentation play a song that expresses the sense of Christian community which you have just discussed. This song should also serve as a "mood setter" to help the young people enter the retreat with seriousness. You may wish to dim the lights and light a candle in the center of the group.

5:20 P.M.

Talk by an older teenager or young adult.

Topic: The Need for Community. The speaker, hopefully a teenager himself or herself, should share in this talk on a personal level with the group. The need for belonging, acceptance, and community should be contrasted with the destructive elements of isolation and alienation. The importance of friendship could be emphasized—again, personal examples from the speaker's experience are crucial for the talk to be effective. The speaker should end the talk by encouraging the group to take the risk to get to know each other better during this Twilight Retreat in order to develop a little deeper level of trust and community. Their year together will then be more meaningful. The talk could end with another recorded song.

5:40 P.M.

In the small group(s) do exercise #1 for the Twilight Retreat in the Journal.

6:20 P.M.

Supper/free time.

6:50 P.M.

Talk by an older teenager or young adult.

Topic: The Power of God Within. This talk focuses on the theological reality that God's life is within us due to our baptism. We can call upon this inner reality to comfort us, assure us, guide us, and support us in difficult times. A suggested scripture reference for the talk is the beginning two chapters of the First Epistle of Peter. The speaker needs to speak very personally about his or her own interior relationship with Christ and provide personal examples of how that relationship has sustained him or her in trying times. To close the talk, the speaker should select an appropriate song.

7:15 P.M.

Small groups do exercise #2 in Journal for this Twilight Retreat.

7:55 P.M.

Break

8:00 P.M.

Closing Prayer Circle. If the floor is carpeted, have all gather, seated on it in a circle. If it is not carpeted, pull your chairs into a close circle. Dim the lights and put a candle and crucifix in the center of the group. Play an opening song. As leader, share a short spontaneous prayer thanking the Lord for the Twilight Retreat and the deepening of community that has occurred. Ask him to bless this bonding of friendships throughout the year. Then tell the group you are going to take the crucifix, the symbol of our faith, and pass it around the group. Each should gaze at it briefly and make a prayer either silently or aloud to the group. (You should then pass it to your two speakers first, asking them to pray aloud so as to encourage the rest of the group and also to demonstrate how it is done.)

When the crucifix has been passed around the entire group, place it back in the center next to the candle. Then ask everyone to join hands as a sign of community and pray aloud together the Lord's Prayer. Conclude by playing another recorded song.

8:30 P.M.
Conclusion

SESSION 3: Love of Neighbor

"If I have not charity, says the Apostle, I am nothing. Whatever my privilege, service, or even virtue, if I have not charity I gain nothing. Charity is superior to all the virtues. It is the first of the theological virtues: 'So faith, hope, charity abide, these three. But the greatest of these is charity'" (CCC #1826).

> **"You have heard that is was said, 'An eye for an eye and a tooth for a tooth.' But I say to you, Do not resist an evildoer. But if anyone strikes you on the right cheek, turn the other also; and if anyone wants to sue you and take your coat, give your cloak as well; and if anyone forces you to go one mile, go also the second mile. Give to everyone who begs from you, and do not refuse anyone who wants to borrow from you.**
>
> **"You have heard that it was said, 'You shall love your neighbor and hate your enemy.' But I say to you, Love your enemies and pray for those who persecute you, so that you may be children of your Father in heaven; for he makes his sun rise on the evil and on the good, and sends rain on the righteous and on the unrighteous. For if you love those who love you, what reward do you have? Do not even the tax collectors do the same? And if you greet only your brothers and sisters, what more are you doing than others? Do not even the Gentiles do the same? Be perfect, therefore, as your heavenly Father is perfect."**
> **(Matthew 5:38–48)**

Under Jewish law a person could sue another for stealing his shirt, which was a longer garment than our shirts of today. It was either the tunic, a long shirt worn next to the body, or a cloak to give protection from the cold and the rain. Basically, in these examples Jesus is rejecting a custom of revenge in the ancient Near East. But we know that the gospel was written for all people and holds a message for us here and now.

Not many of us are going to do the things mentioned in this passage. However, there are all sorts of ways that young people can translate these examples into their own lives. What about walking away from a fight rather than retaliating with physical violence? What about lending money to a friend? What about running an errand for someone twice in the same day? And what about doing something or going somewhere with a friend, even if we don't particularly care to, simply to allow them their preference?

This is a very difficult passage, both in terms of understanding what it means and in the challenge it presents. We see from this reading that to be a good Christian demands tougher things than getting out of bed to go to church on Sunday morning.

We are fortunate to have several verbs in the English language that express attraction toward something or someone. The most common are the verbs "to love" and "to like." The Greek verb that is used in this passage, telling us to love others, is not the same verb Matthew would have chosen if he were talking about the love of a married couple or the love between two friends. In this passage Jesus is telling us that as his followers, we should wish all people well and no one harm. He isn't saying that we have to like everyone we meet in an emotional way. He is saying, however, that as his followers we must treat all with whom we come in contact with kindness. This is the theological virtue of charity.

We should not think of the word enemy as though it were some military battalion standing on a distant shore with guns pointed at us. Enemy is perhaps too strong a word to suggest what is really meant here. Jesus is simply talking about people with whom we find it difficult to relate, or those who mistreat us in some way. Therefore, an enemy in this sense could be a brother or sister, a classmate, an associate at work, a teacher, or a parent. Our challenge as true disciples of Jesus Christ is to try to look for the good in everyone and to treat each person with respect, the same way we like to be treated by others. While we cannot always change the things we find distasteful in the personalities of other people, we can change our own attitudes and behavior. It isn't always easy to be kind, even to people we like. This is often the case because we experience a variety of moods. Sometimes we just feel irritable and out of sorts without really knowing why. At other times some small physical problem like a headache or lack of sleep will affect our behavior toward others.

Another problem with loving people is that our love is not always returned. Ask your teens if they ever did something kind for somebody close to them who didn't seem grateful? They may be able to remember times when their loving actions or words were not appreciated. Poets and authors have given a title to this experience, called "unrequited love." St. Vincent de Paul is reputed to have said that the truest form of charity is when the hand you feed slaps you.

A third problem is the matter of universal love. Many of us feel very compassionate and sympathetic when we see war victims on television or hear news reports of starving children. We might think how easy it must be to love and care for such people. The fact is, however, that we really don't know these people whom we pity. We cannot love what we do not know. And knowing a human being usually entails discovering—among qualities we admire—a few traits we find irksome. This is true between friends, even between husbands and wives. Love at a distance is often much easier than love up close.

Teenagers tend to be very realistic and critical of adults who fall short of their ideals. But while they easily can ruminate how the people in the world should love each other and accept each other, they are seldom self-critical about their own thoughtlessness and unloving behavior. Reflection upon this gospel provides an opportunity for some real soul-searching in this most crucial dimension of Christian life.

JOURNAL EXERCISE

Do Exercise #1, "How Far Will You Go?" and Exercise #2, "Examine Your Heart" in the Journal, Session 3. If your group is not mature enough or secure enough as a forming group to complete Exercise #2, do the "Self in Community Symbol" instead. **Note: If you opt for the "Self in Community Symbol," you will need either crayons or magic markers for this session.**

DISCUSSION QUESTIONS

1. Is there someone in your life you need to forgive?

2. If so, what is blocking forgiveness within you?

SESSION 4: The Final Judgment

"...It is summed up in the Golden Rule, 'Whatever you wish that men would do to you, do so to them; this is the law and the prophets.' The entire Law of the Gospel is contained in the 'new commandment' of Jesus, to love one another as he has loved us" (CCC #1970).

"When the Son of Man comes in his glory, and all the angels with him, then he will sit on the throne of his glory. All the nations will be gathered before him, and he will separate people one from another as a shepherd separates the sheep from the goats, and he will put the sheep at his right hand and the goats at the left. Then the king will say to those at his right hand, 'Come, you that are blessed by my Father, inherit the kingdom prepared for you from the foundation of the world; for I was hungry and you gave me food, I was thirsty and you gave me something to drink, I was a stranger and you welcomed me, I was naked and you gave me clothing, I was sick and you took care of me, I was in prison and you visited me.' Then the righteous will answer him, 'Lord, when was it that we saw you hungry and gave you food, or thirsty and gave you something to drink? And when was it that we saw you a stranger and welcomed you, or naked and gave you clothing? And when was it that we saw you sick or in prison and visited you?' And the king will answer them, 'Truly I tell you, just as you did it to one of the least of these who are members of my family, you did it to me.' Then he will say to those at his left hand, 'You that are accursed, depart from me into the eternal fire prepared for the devil and his angels; for I was hungry and you gave me no food, I was thirsty and you gave me nothing to drink, I was a stranger and you did not welcome me, naked and you did not give me clothing, sick and in prison and you did not visit me.' Then they also will answer, 'Lord, when was it that we saw you hungry or thirsty or a stranger or naked or sick or in prison, and did not take care of you?' Then he will answer them, 'Truly I tell you, just as you did not do it to one of the least of these, you did not do it to me.' And these will go away into eternal punishment, but the righteous into eternal life." (Matthew 25:31–46)

In many ways we might consider this chapter in Matthew's Gospel the most important of all, for in this chapter Jesus describes very clearly a capsule version of what the whole of Christian life ought to be. It is the core of the moral teaching of Jesus and the source of what the church calls the "corporal works of mercy" (see Journal, Session 10 for a list). Until recently, many Catholics thought that salvation depends only on attendance at Sunday Mass and the purity of one's sexual life. Yet here in this depiction of the final judgment, the New Testament is saying that, in the last analysis, love determines whether a person is good or bad.

As St. John of the Cross said: "In the evening of our life we shall all be judged according to our love." Of course, this love includes the love of God. But Jesus has already told us that we can best show our love for God by loving our fellow human beings. Let there be no misunderstanding here. To fail to participate in Sunday Mass with the Christian community can indeed be a failure to love both God and people. And, of course, to take advantage of another person sexually shows an obvious lack of love. What we are trying to say is that the third and sixth commandments simply do not exhaust the breadth of the Christian life.

Most of us, when we think of sin, think of doing something wrong. In technical terms, we call these sins of "commission." But take a look at the reasons why "the King" in the gospel story sends some people off to eternal punishment. Every single accusation made against them consists of an action they failed to do. These we call sins of "omission." Sin, for most of us, is largely what we don't do, opportunities for good that we could have seized and chose not to. Another helpful gospel story on the topic of sins of omission is the story of the Good Samaritan found in Luke 10:29–37.

If you have time to reflect on it during this session it would be helpful (or we suggest that it be read during the week). Suggested follow-up questions could include who it is in your own life you are "passing by" and why it is that you are doing so (laziness, apathy, envy, fear, self-centeredness, etc.).

Here is a quote from Michael Warren, a pioneer in Roman Catholic youth ministry, in an address he delivered to the leaders of the successful teenage retreat movement called T.E.C. (Teenagers Encounter Christ):

> I have been concerned about the vision or portrait
> of Jesus being presented in many different programs
> for middle-class youth. This Jesus tends to be a middle-class
> Jesus, representing the dominant concerns of the moderately
> well-off and privileged. The dominant concern of the
> middle-class tends to be greater comfort,
> and thus the middle-class Jesus is presented as
> the one who comforts. Overlooked is the Jesus
> who not only comforted but who also confronted
> and challenged, Jesus the upsetter. The middle-class
> Jesus is the "Man For Others"; the middle-class Jesus
> is the Man for us. If there is any challenge offered by
> such a presentation of Jesus, it is the challenge of
> accepting him as a sign of God's love for us.
> Obviously it is essential to understand Jesus as God-with-us
> and as God's special gift to us. Accepting Jesus
> as God's love embodied is an important first step
> on the road to discipleship. Yet, to go no further is
> to remain with a middle-class and ultimately false
> image of Jesus. The gospels remind us in many ways
> that Jesus offers us not so much the Jesus-Hug, as a
> call for ourselves to embrace the poor and the weak
> and those who do not fit. In the gospels, Jesus continually
> calls attention, not to himself, but to the social situations
> that needed to be changed and to the people who
> suffered in these social situations, the poor.
> (From "The Renewal of T.E.C.
and Other Youth Retreats")

At the same time we adults need to go easy on adolescents with respect to thinking of others simply because this emotional maturity is developmentally limited. The twenty-fifth chapter of Matthew's Gospel can be a helpful source of meditation in encouraging teenagers to begin to think of the other person and to illustrate to them how pivotal unselfishness is to salvation in the Christian life. Most of us have forgotten that to be a teenager is to be constantly in front of an imagined audience who are inspecting us up and down and judging every aspect of our appearance and every movement we make. The adolescent is a person generally very focused upon himself or herself and one knows that one is passing into maturity when one's focus shifts toward another and the process of assuming a unique identity gains momentum. So some degree of egocentricity is normal to adolescence. However, there can be degrees out of proportion which can often be traced to low self-esteem. A temper tantrum is an obvious giveaway of a strong degree of self-centeredness.

Because adolescents are so concerned with the reaction of others to themselves and constantly envisage their imaginary audience, it is a difficult challenge to talk about their being concerned with feeding the hungry, clothing the naked, and visiting the sick in the concrete (as opposed to the theoretical). Mother Theresa, in the video "Everyone, Everywhere," asks this question: "Do you really know the 'poor' in your own house, in your own family, in your own community?" ("Everyone Everywhere," Franciscan Communications, St. Anthony Messenger Press).

JOURNAL EXERCISE
Do Exercise #1 "The Final Judgment" and Exercise #2 "E-mail to Jesus" in the Journal, Session 4.

DISCUSSION QUESTIONS
1.   Do you think that loneliness is a type of poverty?

2.   Do you see followers of Jesus as responsible to alleviate the loneliness of others?

SESSION 5: Selfishness

"Every practice that reduces persons to nothing more than a means of profit enslaves man, leading to idolizing money, and contributes to the spread of atheism. 'You cannot serve both God and mammon'" (CCC #2424).

And he said to them, "Take care! Be on your guard against all kinds of greed; for one's life does not consist in the abundance of possessions." Then he told them a parable: "The land of a rich man produced abundantly. And he thought to himself, 'What should I do, for I have no place to store my crops?' Then he said, 'I will do this: I will pull down my barns and build larger ones, and there I will store all my grain and my goods. And I will say to my soul, 'Soul you have ample goods laid up for many years; relax, eat, drink, and be merry.' But God said to him, 'You fool! This very night your life is being demanded of you. And the things that you have prepared, whose will they be?' So it is with those who store up treasures for themselves but are not rich toward God." (Luke 12:15–21)

In this parable Jesus is telling us that a meaningful life is not the result of an abundance of material riches. This text is very important in our materialistic culture where more and more young people are focusing on economic prosperity as chief among their life's goals. Parents who are legitimately concerned with their children's security can knowingly or unknowingly foster this attitude as well. What is needed today is for young people to have experiences where they discover a deep satisfaction within from experiences other than the acquisition of money or material goods. Hopefully your group itself is a place where they are discovering the joy of mutual sharing. Also, their retreat experiences should contribute to this discovery. Through their community service experience this year they should discover the satisfaction in helping someone less fortunate. Prayer is another way for them to discover real peace. If they have enough of these types of experiences in their youth, these should serve as touchstones as they grow older and begin to be more pressured and lured by economic gain.

Jesus says in verse 15 to "avoid greed in all its forms." It is very challenging to talk to teenagers (who are still in the process of building an ego) about being non-possessive. At many levels it is probably psychologically next to impossible for them to be liberated from the shackles of greed. You have to have an ego or a sense of self to be able to give up your ego—and teenagers are midway in this process. But what we can do is to hold up this gospel as the ideal for which Christians should strive. The memory of this group, or at least of this concept, should serve as a reference point as they grow older in a world so preoccupied with prosperity and economic advancement.

In psychological terms, it is very difficult for teenagers to think of "letting go." An individual needs to possess an ego before he or she is able to surrender it. And yet even though we recognize this process of achieving a sense of self as healthy and necessary, we can still hold out to them the Christian ideal of selflessness. Many of the teachings of Jesus call for a human and spiritual maturity which we only achieve gradually in life. And yet we need to teach the stories of the gospel and the ideals of Jesus to our children so that his message will echo in their consciousness as their own individual life stories unfold.

Roman Catholicism has traditionally held that there are seven "capital" sins which are the prime sources of all sin. These inclinations are: pride, lust, anger, gluttony, envy, sloth, and covetousness. *Covetousness* is an older English word, not much in usage today, which means an inordinate or unreasonable desire for what one does not possess. A form of covetousness is avarice or greed—the focus of this parable—that is the sin in which material goods and wealth become ends in themselves.

This problem of greed and materialistic self-centeredness is so obviously dominant today that this topic of unselfishness requires as much attention as possible. The media and the Internet prey upon the youth culture and incessantly invite teenagers to endless selfishness. The ethic of many adults only compounds adolescent egocentrism by supporting the concept that economic gain should be the reason why a person chooses a career. A self-centered lifestyle has become quite acceptable in North America, even within the Christian community. It is difficult for many young people to see beyond its superficial lure. Throughout the course of your group's sessions you are teaching teenagers to think about other values than the world's values—those of Jesus. You are helping them to penetrate beneath the surface of things and to discover realities which are enduring.

Of course the problem of selfishness extends beyond the material. We can be selfish with our time, our talents, the people whom we love. Reflection upon the phenomenon of jealousy can be very helpful for teenagers. Insecurity and the problems that result from a low self-image are usually at the root of human jealousy. But it takes time, discussion, and assistance for young people to see beyond the purported reasons for their jealousies. If time permits during this session, you might ask the group to talk about their problems with jealousy as an extension of the topic of unselfishness. (Jealousy will also be discussed in the session on the Ten Commandments.)

JOURNAL EXERCISE
Do Exercise #1, "My Barn," and Exercise #2, "Sentence Completers," in the Journal, Session 5.

DISCUSSION QUESTIONS
1. Is your lifestyle simple or extravagant?

2. Do you ever spend money wastefully? How?

SESSION 6
PART A
Suffering

"The world we live in often seems very far from the one promised us by faith. Our experiences of evil and suffering, injustice and death, seem to contradict the Good News; they can shake our faith and become a temptation against it" (CCC #164).

> "No one can serve two masters; for a slave will either hate the one and love the other or be devoted to the one and despise the other. You cannot serve God and wealth.
>
> "Therefore I tell you, do not worry about your life, what you will eat or what you will drink, or about your body, what you will wear. Is not life more than food, and the body more than clothing? Look at the birds of the air; they neither sow nor reap nor gather into barns, and yet your heavenly Father feeds them. Are not you of more value than they? And can any of you by worrying add a single hour to your span of life? And why do you worry about clothing? Consider the lilies of the field, how they grow; they neither toil nor spin, yet I tell you, even Solomon in all his glory was not clothed like one of these. But if God so clothes the grass of the field, which is alive today and tomorrow is thrown into the oven, will he not much more clothe you—you of little faith? Therefore do not worry, saying, 'What will we eat?' or 'What will we drink?' or 'What will we wear?' For it is the Gentiles who strive for all these things; and indeed your heavenly Father knows that you need all these things. But strive first for the kingdom of God and his righteousness, and all these things will be given to you as well.
>
> "So do not worry about tomorrow, for tomorrow will bring worries of its own. Today's trouble is enough for today." (Matthew 6:24–34)

The Greek verb for *worry* in this gospel passage is a very strong word, meaning "to be anxious." "Do not worry" here does not mean "don't plan" or "don't be careful." In this passage Jesus is encouraging his followers not to be overly concerned about food and clothing and the necessities of life. How many of us are concerned with things that aren't necessary for human survival, even to the point of getting nervous about them?

This chapter has a real message for today. So many people are wrapped up in cares about success and material goods—and not all of them are adults. If Jesus felt it necessary to caution the Jewish people about such things—people whose standard of living was far below ours—can you imagine what he would say to our American culture today? The most consoling line of this text is found at the very end. Seriously, what good does worrying about anything do? Worry certainly never solves problems. In fact, it can often make them worse; it often prevents us from thinking clearly. It is useless to worry, especially about the unknown, because God has promised to take very good care of us.

Sometimes teenagers misinterpret this section of the gospel to mean that passivity is virtuous. It's important to distinguish between inactivity and the inner virtue of trust. Jesus' point is that worry or anxiety cannot speed the growth of plants in the field, add to the beauty of the birds in the sky, or add a day to our lifetime. While there may be psychological roots and insecurity to human anxiety, faith in God's care for us should contribute to the lessening of worry, and over time help the Christian to cultivate a posture of faith that leads to a life of inner freedom and peace. It is to this that this gospel section invites young people.

This discussion of anxiety may lead to a discussion of the wider question of suffering. Human suffering is an inexhaustible mystery. Because this mystery is part and parcel of the human condition, Jesus spoke to us about it. The following reflections might help you to better discuss the meaning of suffering with your group.

1. Does God actually send certain sufferings to certain people? Does he plot our misery? Some people may think so, because of early childhood experiences or because of remarks by parents and teachers. But such a concept does not square with what Jesus has revealed. The God whom Jesus revealed is Love itself. A loving father never sends deliberate misery. We suffer both in mind and body because of the vulnerability of the human condition (that is, because of original sin). We certainly do not suffer because God likes to see us in pain.

2. Do we suffer in this life for our sins? The answer to this question is both yes and no. We do not suffer for our sins in the way the ancient Jews thought. For example, when the ancient Jews were struck by famine, they would interpret the disaster as a punishment from God for misbehavior. This primitive way of thinking was too simple; God does not act in that way. To put it in more concrete terms, God doesn't see to it that we stub our toe after we've said a swear word. We do suffer in this life for our sins, however, in the sense that sin and unkindness have their own way of bringing misery into our lives. The saying is true that we begin our heaven or hell here on earth.

3. Of what value is human suffering? This question can be approached from many angles. The value does not lie in the suffering itself but in the attitude with which we approach it. Two axioms apply here. The first axiom is: When we pray to be delivered from suffering, God often changes us rather than the situation. The second axiom is St. Augustine's piece of advice: "...to accept what I must, change what I can, and have the wisdom to know the difference."

Another note of wisdom is to be found in the opening greeting of St. Paul's second epistle to the Corinthians. Paul tells the people of Corinth to bless God who comforts us in our sorrows so that we can help others to bear patiently what we have suffered. Of course, the highest value of human suffering is that of serving the good of another human being. Jesus' own death for us is a witness to that.

JOURNAL EXERCISE
Do Exercise "Worry Spectrum" in the Journal, Session 6.

DISCUSSION QUESTIONS
1. Do you ever blame God for something he didn't create or cause?

2. Do you see yourself as responsible for or contributing to any human suffering?

PART B
The Mystery of Death

"But about that day and hour no one knows, neither the angels of heaven, nor the Son, but only the Father. For as the days of Noah were, so will be the coming of the Son of Man. For as in those days before the flood they were eating and drinking, marrying and giving in marriage, until the day Noah entered the ark, and they knew nothing until the flood came and swept them all away, so too will be the coming of the Son of Man. Then two will be in the field; one will be taken and one will be left. Two women will be grinding meal togehter; one will be taken and one will be left. Keep awake therefore, for you do not know on what day your Lord is coming. But understand this: if the owner of the house had known in what part of the night the thief was coming, he would have stayed awake and would not have let his house be broken into. Therefore you also must be ready, for the Son of Man is coming at an unexpected hour." (Matthew 24:36–44)

North American society shields its people from the harsh reality of death. We do this in a number of ways. We are, for example, one of the few countries in the world which separates the aging from the young, instead of having grandparents, uncles, and aunts live with their families. We have created a pattern of social behavior whereby old people are shuffled off to nursing homes and housing for the elderly. In so doing, we run the risk of shielding our children from being in touch with the process of aging. We also limit children's exposure to the experience of death. Many sociologists feel that this isolation of the old from the young does harm to both. It creates in the young an unwarranted fear of growing old, and it creates in aging persons a morbid attitude toward their own impending deaths.

Another means that American culture uses to avoid the issue of death is evasive vocabulary. For instance, we don't say that a man is dead, we say he has passed away. Or sympathy cards will attempt to subdue the issue by saying such things as: "He has only gone away for a while." The funeral parlor is another place where the stark reality of a person's death is often glossed over. The final point is our inability as a people to discuss death openly. Many mothers and fathers never mention death to their children. Doctors and nurses, surprisingly enough, often fail to discuss it even with their very sick patients. All of us know from experience that when people around us refuse to discuss an important issue, we become more curious about it, and often more frightened.

The discussion of death may easily lead to a discussion of eternal life. Many of our ideas of heaven were rooted in our mind during childhood. We seldom outgrow these ideas, nor is it necessary that we should. Many of us have mental images of clouds in the sky, or perhaps even of angels flying around playing harps.

Regarding your own mental image, ask yourself this question: "Do I picture heaven as an interesting way of existing, or do I think of it as boring?" If you answer that your picture of heaven is boring, you can be sure that your idea does not correspond to the same eternal prize Jesus spoke of. Scripture tells us: **"What no eye has seen, nor ear heard, nor the human heart conceived, what God has prepared for those who love him"** (1 Corinthians 2:9).

It is probably best to start off by trying to stop thinking of heaven as a geographical place. In Jesus' time, many people had the idea that after death the human being was consigned to a place beneath the ground called *Sheol*. Sheol, a lagoon-like sort of existence, was not a place of reward or punishment. It was simply a place to go after the human heart stopped beating. Trying to correct this notion, Jesus points to his eternal life as upward. Therefore, he uses the example of the sky. He is trying, in the gospel, to show that the eternal life his followers will enjoy will not be like Sheol. But what will it be like? The late noted Catholic author, Mary Reed Newland, once explained heaven in a very beautiful way. She spoke of addressing a little embryo within a mother's womb and saying to it: "Hey, come on out of there. Let's go to the beach today. We'll walk along the shore; we'll build sand castles and buy ice cream, and go swimming! We'll have a wonderful time." And that if she could respond, the little babe within the mother's womb would say: "Shore, sand, ice cream, swim? I have no idea what you're talking about. I'm going to stay right here where it's nice and snug and warm." And that we could respond: "Oh, if only you knew how glorious life is out here!" At birth, of course, the baby is expelled from the mother's womb, and his eyes are open to a glorious new world.

There is a comparison between the birth of the child and the extension of our lives in heaven. If the saints in heaven could speak so that we could hear them, they might say such things as: "Oh hurry and join us! We're having a wonderful time where we are." And we, in typical human fashion, would respond: "Oh no, we don't want to go. We don't want to come yet. We're too secure. We're enjoying our lives here on earth too much." But when we have our second birth, when we are expelled from the womb of this life, our eyes will behold new and glorious sights. An important footnote: Before engaging in this discussion, be aware that some teenagers in your group may have experienced the death of a grandparent or parent, or the death or suicide of a friend or classmate. This discussion could trigger a strong emotional reaction on the part of some member(s) of your group. This would probably be a very healthy reaction, so it is not to be feared or discouraged. But you need as the leader to be prepared for it. It might be good to query the group before you begin about who has experienced the death of someone close. Some group member may be too vulnerable to participate in this discussion because of a recent or impending loss.

JOURNAL EXERCISE
Do Exercise "My Own Eulogy" in the Journal, Session 6.

DISCUSSION QUESTIONS
1. Do you think very often about your individual death?

2. Do you think your generation will experience global destruction? Do you think about it very often?

SESSION 7
PART A
Prayer

"The Beatitudes are at the heart of Jesus' preaching...the Beatitudes respond to the natural desire for happiness. This desire is of divine origin. God has placed it in the human heart in order to draw men to the One alone who can fulfill it" (CCC #1716/1718).

"Ask, and it will be given you; search, and you will find; knock, and the door will be opened for you. For everyone who asks receives, and everyone who searches finds, and for everyone who knocks, the door will be opened. Is there anyone among you who, if your child asks for bread, will give a stone? Or if the child asks for a fish, will give it a snake? If you then, you are evil, know how to give good gifts to your children, how much more will your Father in heaven give good things to those who ask him!" (Matthew 7:7–11)

The most important part about this passage is: when you ask for something in prayer, do you really believe you will receive it? If you do not believe that Jesus really answers prayers, ask yourself: When I pray for something, do I pray as a sort of last resort, figuring that it probably won't help but at least it couldn't hurt? What attitude do you have deep down at the bottom of your heart? Do you have the attitude that Jesus really is going to help you, or is your deepest expectation that he won't? A second question to ask yourself is: Am I persistent when I pray? The fact that Matthew uses the three verbs, ask, seek, knock, shows very clearly that prayers are not always answered immediately. Patience and perseverance are often required of us. A close examination of the New Testament miracles tells us that Jesus always demands faith in his ability to cure, and sometimes persistence in this faith as well.

Young people need to learn to take these words of Jesus and understand them in a spiritual way in the context of a friendship. We are in relationship with God and so of course he will respond to our needs. But, just as in human relationships, we need to give God the freedom to respond as he sees fit. Our trust, our faith is that he will hear our prayer of petition, especially if we persist in it.

School work is a good place to start to discuss "prayers of petition" with young people. Ronald Goldman concludes that children from age thirteen to seventeen show an increased desire to be helped with schoolwork by God (*Religious Thinking from Childhood to Adolescence,* London, Routledge and Kegan Paul, 1964, p. 240). If teenagers, for example, tell you that they blame God for not helping them pass an exam, you might take advantage of the moment to ask some searching questions: Did they study as hard as they should have? You can explain that passivity is not a posture for prayer, and that we must work toward human solutions of the same things for which we are praying. Is this one test the issue, or is it attitude toward study that needs a conversion? Does nervousness inhibit them, and is it really peace of mind during exams that is their deeper need? Do they need a deeper spirit of self-discipline? Can they use this failure to teach themselves about their deeper human need? God is interested in their total development as a person. Perhaps that should be the focus of their next prayer.

By reflecting with the adolescent on the nature of their prayer, adults can often make brief remarks that can help expand the horizon of how to pray and for what. Of course, they should not scoff at youth when concrete situational change (e.g., boy-girl relationship) is perceived as an answer to prayer. It just may be. If it isn't, there is no harm done either. It's when prayers are not answered in a concrete way that the issues are raised and the spiritual guidance of an adult is needed.

"Prayer does not change God, but it changes the one who offers it" (Soren Kierkegaard). Young people might at first read this sentence as an adult's way of skirting the question: Does God really answer prayer? But indeed it is not. Persons who have persisted in prayer of petition have discovered this experience even though they may not be able to articulate the change that has occurred within them. To persist in asking the Lord for help in the face of an "unanswered" prayer is to go on a spiritual adventure.

But perhaps more important than talking to God is listening to God speak to us. This he does if we still ourselves enough interiorly to listen to his promptings and inspirations. If your group is not accustomed to the practice of passive silent prayer, use the end of this session as a time for them to experience it.

Meditation is a term we give to thinking in silent prayer. One of the best things to do while meditating is to keep a religious book or the Bible in front of us—or a crucifix, a candle, or holy picture (or even a tree outside a window)—something we can focus on. Meditating slowly on the written word helps us to focus our attention. In the past sessions we have been doing a sort of group meditation by thinking about the gospel passages and applying them to our personal lives. We can meditate on scripture, prayers, poems, experiences—anything that moves us into a conversation with the Lord.

Contemplation, a term we sometimes use interchangeably with meditation, has a slightly different meaning. It involves a suspension of the thought process. The stress is not on thinking but on letting go of thought. It is being absorbed in silence so that God can speak to us. Sometimes it happens for brief intervals in prayer when we have quieted ourselves sufficiently. Teenagers living in today's frenetic culture, always surrounded by music and noise, need to be taught how to pray in a more spiritually mature way. The following are some practical suggestions for you to share with them on this important topic:

1. Choose a quiet place to pray where you will not be disturbed.

2. Turn off the music, pagers, and cell phones. Only use music as preliminary to prayer—perhaps a certain song helps you to calm down.

3. Pray at a specific time of day (e.g., upon rising).

4. Decide to pray for a definite period of time on a consistent basis (like five minutes). This discipline protects your time for prayer.

5. As for posture, we advise "comfortable, but not too comfortable." Do not lie on the bed. Don't slouch, and keep your backbone straight.

JOURNAL EXERCISE

Do Exercise "My Personal Prayer Descriptions" in the Journal, Session 7.

DISCUSSION QUESTIONS

1. Do you consider prayer a joy, a relief, or a chore?

2. Do you see any value in having a regular time to pray each day? What time of day would you choose and why?

PART B
The Beatitudes

When Jesus saw the crowds, he went up the mountain; and after he sat down, his disciples came to him. Then he began to speak, and taught them, saying:

"Blessed are the poor in spirit, for theirs is the kingdom of heaven.

"Blessed are those who mourn, for they will be comforted.

"Blessed are the meek, for they will inherit the earth.

"Blessed are those who hunger and thirst for righteousness, for they will be filled.

"Blessed are the merciful, for they will receive mercy.

"Blessed are the pure in heart, for they will see God.

"Blessed are the peacemakers, for they will be called children of God.

"Blessed are those who are persecuted for righteousness' sake, for theirs is the kingdom of heaven.

"Blessed are you when people revile you and persecute you and utter all kinds of evil against you falsely on my account.Rejoice and be glad, for your reward is great in heaven, for in the same way they persecuted the prophets who were before you."
(Matthew 5:1–12)

Scripture scholars consider this short section from Jesus' sermon on the mount to be a summary of Christian living. They are called the *beatitudes*. Let us take each of them and comment.

1. "Blessed are the poor in spirit...." There are two ways of being poor. In this early chapter of his Gospel, Matthew is not talking about poverty that comes from having no money or living in destitute conditions. The type of poverty that Matthew says brings true happiness is a different kind indeed. For we all know that to be without material possessions is no guarantee of a joyous life. Perhaps a better word to substitute for "poor" in this passage would be dependent. We all know how good it is to be dependent on people, such as friends or family. We may not often think about experiences of being dependent, yet we have these experiences all the time. For example, if it were not for our alarm clock, or our mother, or spouse, we would not have awakened this morning on time. Do we ever stop to realize that small area of dependency in our lives? Do we stop to think how dependent we are on the food that we eat each day to keep our bodies in good health? In our modern society we take for granted so many things like electricity, computers, the telephone, the television, the DVD player, the CD player, cell phones, and pagers. Matthew is talking about a type of *spiritual* dependency.

2. "Blessed are those who mourn...." This beatitude doesn't mean that Jesus is masochistic. Suffering is to be avoided as much as is humanly possible. But a certain amount of suffering is intrinsic to existence. This beatitude implies that suffering is not in vain and that in the "next life" we will be comforted.

3. "Blessed are the meek...." Meekness is humility and humility is truth. When we receive praise for something—for example, if we have cooked a good meal or hit a home run or achieved advancement at work—we should not deny the compliment but accept it graciously. After all, who gave us the eyes to read the recipe or to see the ball coming at us? We are not proud of our eyesight; we are simply grateful for being blessed with it. False humility is revealed when people deny the good within them or the good that they have achieved.

4. "Blessed are they who hunger and thirst for righteousness...." God's will is not something that we can ever get a handle on or finally discover. All that we can do is try to discover who we are and what our own deepest desires are. God wants us to know ourselves, appreciate ourselves, and follow our own hearts. One could almost say that God's will is my will, not in the selfish sense, but in the sense of the summons to truth and goodness I can discover within. The kingdom of God is both within us and around every corner we turn in good faith. Just wanting and trying to do what we feel is right is to do his will. It's so simple; God is Love and if we live lovingly, God will live in us and we will live in him.

5. "Blessed are the merciful...." This does not mean that Jesus wants us to become a doormat for other people or not stand up for our own rights. Mercy is a choice that helps us to be kind. It is inner strength that helps us to sometimes not interfere, not talk back or hurl insults, not demand our own way. Meekness and mercy both mean simply giving in to the needs of other people, not constantly or totally, but certainly beyond the limits of ordinary human selfishness.

6. "Blessed are the pure in heart...." While sexual purity is certainly a Christian value of the highest order, Jesus is talking here about our inner intentions, our singleness of vision, the virtue of simplicity.

7. "Blessed are the peacemakers...." We understand this both in a relational way (being a peacemaker or reconciler in one's family or among one's friends) and also today in a global way. To work for peace and justice is the responsibility of every follower of Jesus.

8. "Blessed are those who are persecuted...." Jesus is not saying that persecution is a happy situation or good. He is saying that all of these statements of his are foolishness in terms of the values of the world. The world's values are not the same as Christian values. Each of these beatitudes is a paradox, a seeming contradiction, in that what the world deems undesirable will, in Jesus' words, bring happiness or blessedness. We can really see in the last beatitude how counter-cultural Jesus intended his message to be. Brother Roger Schutz of Taizé remarked: "In a world where new technologies are making possible advances never before imagined, it is important not to neglect fundamental values of the inner life: compassion, simplicity of heart and life, humble trust in God, serene joy" (Taizé Youth Meeting, Budapest, Hungary, Dec. 28, 2001).

JOURNAL EXERCISE
Do exercise "Beatitudinal Profile" in the Journal, Session 7.

DISCUSSION QUESTIONS
1. The pursuit of happiness is part of the American dream. Do you think that happiness itself can really be pursued?

2. In what way, as Jesus seems to be saying, is happiness found?

> **Individual interviews discussed in the introductory session, "Precatechumenate," should occur between this session and the "Rite of Choice."**

CATECHUMENATE

Modeled on the R.C.I.A., we are calling the next phase of our confirmation process the *Catechumenate*. Its purpose is to form the candidates in living the Christian life and deepening their faith. While most of this period is devoted to formation, the next four sessions will include a basic review of fundamental Roman Catholic doctrine. For some of the teenagers the doctrinal portion will be a review of material already learned. For others it may be new material. These latter individuals may need some special attention outside of the weekly session time.

While the confirmation preparation process is not primarily an academic enterprise, we do feel it appropriate to give one written or oral test at the end of the three-week study (a sample test you may wish to use is included). It is necessary for the candidates to know the Ten Commandments, the seven sacraments, the Apostles' Creed, liturgical seasons, the precepts of the church, and some very basic religious terminology. Three fundamental means will be employed for this formation period: insistence that the candidates participate in the liturgical life of the parish; the development of community through the group sessions; the service project and the Parent-Youth Mini-Retreat. Catechesis has a fourfold shape: doctrine, Christian living or morality, ministry and prayer. This period of Catechumenate begins with a parish celebration of the Rite of Choice, discussed in the introduction to the **I Have Chosen You** process. "Maturing in Faith: The Challenge of Adolescent Catechesis" (published by the National Federation for Catholic Youth Ministry in 1986) states that the aim of adolescent catechesis is "to sponsor youth toward maturity in Catholic Christian faith as a living reality." In our sacramental preparation process we are constantly attempting to embrace those two prongs: helping young people to grow as human beings and also passing on to them the riches and graces of their Roman Catholic tradition.

A footnote about the test: If you choose to administer it, don't use it as a threat that those who fail the test cannot be confirmed. Remember, we do not achieve a sacrament; a sacrament is a gift of God. If some candidates fail the test, retest and retest until the material has been retained.

Celebration of the Rite of Choice

(Preceded by a week of interviews discussed in the introductory section. Materials needed: tapers for each candidate and a paschal candle)

Several weeks before confirmation, in accord with the R.C.I.A. model, a "rite of enrollment" will be celebrated in the context of a Sunday liturgy. This event symbolizes the parish community choosing or electing certain individuals to receive the sacrament of confirmation. The Rite of Choice, on the other hand, signifies the individual young person's choice himself or herself to be fully initiated into the Catholic faith. It provides an opportunity for the parish community to be connected to the celebration of confirmation at an early stage. Parents as well as sponsors should be requested to attend. The candidates with their group leader(s) should process into the church together and sit together as a group visible to the community. The celebrant should open the liturgy with words of welcome to the candidates and their families. He should also pray for them during the Mass, particularly highlighting their needs during the Prayer of the Faithful.

At an appropriate point during the liturgy, after the gospel or after the reception of the Eucharist or before the final blessing, the "Rite of Choice" should be celebrated. Of course the more vibrant the entire liturgy with music and liturgical decorations (flowers, banners, etc.), the more meaningful and memorable the event will be. A lighted paschal candle in the sanctuary enhances the occasion.

RITE OF CHOICE

Presentation of Candidates (by D.R.E. or youth minister, president of the pastoral council, or you, the catechist): Stand facing the pastor in sanctuary.

"Father (pastor's name)_____, I present to you the members of our parish community preparing for the sacrament of confirmation. Already having been baptized into Christ they choose today to follow Jesus more closely by entering into a catechetical preparation for this sacrament. To help them in this process they turn to you, our leader, and the parish community of (name of parish)_____ for support, encouragement, and guidance."

Pastor: "Members of this parish community, you have heard the request for our guidance and support. Are you willing to help these young people by your witness of Christian living and by your prayers?"

Congregation: "We are."

Pastor: "Parents and sponsors present here today, are you willing to give that special encouragement these candidates will need from you in their continuing Christian journey?"

Parents and Sponsors: "We are." **[Confirmation candidates now stand]**

Pastor: "Confirmation candidates, do you make a special choice today to embark in a process of intensive catechetical preparation for full initiation into the Catholic faith?

Candidates: "We do."

Pastor: "Do you freely choose to try to follow the gospel teachings which you have been reviewing?

Candidates: "We do."

Pastor: "Do you promise to study, to pray, to serve, and to build community in order to become a young adult witness to Jesus Christ?"

Candidates: "We do."

Pastor: "Take and receive this light from our parish paschal candle [he takes his taper to the paschal candle and extends it to the first candidate who lights the next candidate's, etc., in a "chain-like" fashion] as a symbol of your choice to become a witness to Jesus Christ, the light that has come into this world to dispel the darkness of sin and death. May you burn with love for him and all your brothers and sisters in this world."

(After the last taper has been lit the pastor continues)

"We, the parish of) (name of parish)_____, pledge to support your journey in faith and look forward to the day of your confirmation when you share with us more fully in Christian adulthood." (The congregation applauds)

SESSION 8: The Ten Commandments

"The Ten Commandments state what is required in the love of God and love of neighbor. The first three concern love of God, and the other seven love of neighbor" (CCC #2067).

Our faith is rooted in Judaism. Therefore it is important that our youth have a basic grasp of the Old Testament. Because the ancient Jews were a society, their covenant with God needed to be "fleshed out" in very specific ways. These laws, called the Ten Commandments, undergird Christian morality today. (They are also called the *Decalogue*, which means *word*—the ten "words" God spoke to Moses.) You will notice that the eight Beatitudes are of a higher moral order than the Ten Commandments. But the Commandments are an important part of our heritage and should be both memorized and understood by young Catholics. We will offer here a short commentary on each commandment.

1. I am the LORD your God,....you shall have no other gods before me.

From the time of the Jews, people have had all sorts of false gods which they believed existed, either in some aspects of nature (like the sun) or in some man-made statue or image. God, through Moses, in his first commandment, tried to tell the Jewish people that there was only one true God. The problem for the Jews was that the true God was invisible, whereas a god in nature could be observed as could the graven image. And so it took a new jump of faith for a person in Jewish times to be able to believe in an invisible deity. For us today this commandment also means that we shouldn't put other things before God (like money, pleasure, power, success, possessions, etc.).

2. You shall not make wrongful use of the name of the LORD your God....

In ancient Jewish times the knowledge and use of a person's name was an indication that one was acquainted with the inner depth of that person. Thus, in their thinking, the misuse of God's name was to reduce God to the level of a creature. Swearing, while not appropriate to a follower of Jesus Christ, is not the focus of this commandment. Blasphemy, however, is to intentionally insult or deny the goodness of God.

3. Remember the Sabbath day, and keep it holy.

The Sabbath, for the Jew, was the gift of God to humanity so that people could rest from labors and focus on the spiritual meaning of life. From earliest Christian times Sunday, the day of Christ's resurrection, has been accepted as the Sabbath. While the eucharistic liturgy is not mentioned in the commandment, it is the church's explanation and application of the commandment to "keep holy the Lord's day."

4. Honor your father and your mother....

Children owe their parents respect and obedience. This is not only submission to authority figures, but also a dependence upon them. Teenagers need to be more sensitive to parents, grandparents, stepparents and guardians, and they need to realize that young people are not the only people with feelings. By including these special adults in their life, they are honoring their father and mother. (Note: Do not address your group with the presumption that everyone lives in a two-parent family. There may be a single parent family, stepchildren, foster children, children being raised by a relative, legal guardian, etc.) Teenagers in our society often get the idea that, because peer relationships are more fun and interesting, the family can be dropped or, in a way, forgotten. This is really not fair to those adults who have invested so much love and energy and time and financial resources in their children. It hurts them very much when their teenage children refuse to be present for meals, family gatherings, outings, visits to grandmother, and so forth.

5. You shall not murder.

This commandment underscores respect for life with the Christian perspective that life is a gift of God. The practical implications of this are manifold and include the quality of life. Statements of the American bishops against capital punishment, abortion, building weapons of mass destruction, and ignoring the poor all relate to this commandment. Killing is forbidden based on the fact that a human being does not have dominion over the life of another.

Another way to look at this commandment is to say that murder is wrong. It seems at times in the ancient Jewish world, murder was committed without much forethought. However, there are other ways to "kill" than with a weapon. We can kill with a glance, with a word, with a cutting remark. And so too this commandment asks us to think about our treatment of others, especially those who are different from us by race or age or social status, or those whom we might be prone to pick on. It also asks us to be sensitive to the treatment of members of our own families, where we all know too well each other's points of weakness and vulnerability. Do we take advantage of one another and, in a sense, "kill" each other instead of affirming each other?

6. You shall not commit adultery.

Adultery, a married person having a sexual affair with someone who is not his or her spouse, belies the sacramental commitment of marriage. It is considered a very grave sin. We should also note that cruelty, abuse, disrespect, and lovelessness in marriage are also serious sins. This commandment also has some meaning for those who are not married. The Catholic Church's position is that sexual relations are only permissible between two people who are married to each other. The church doesn't make this rule just to make life more difficult for teenagers who are feeling their sexual energy in a very strong way. Sin, by one definition, is doing something which ultimately hurts you. The church, in its wisdom, the community of believers over the ages, realizes that young people are simply not ready to make the commitment to another person that's involved in the act of sexual intercourse. While physically capable of sex, they are not yet emotionally capable of the commitment it evokes; nor is it fair to a child to be born into a union of two immature young people.

7. You shall not steal.

This commandment involves respect for the rights of other persons to possess material goods. This commandment forbids theft, embezzlement, larceny, looting, and all other forms of robbery. Cheating is also forbidden by this commandment, which has many implications for honest academic and business practices. (Of relevance to this age group is a discussion of the immorality of copying the writing and test answers of others.)

8. You shall not bear false witness against your neighbor.

This commandment teaches us to be truthful and to be respectful of the reputation of other persons. It forbids lying, especially in a way that harms another's good name. Rash judgment (i.e., a negative judgment of others without sufficient reason) is also forbidden. For teenagers their insecurities about themselves often contribute to putting others down. The area to work on is self-image.

9. You shall not covet your neighbor's house...your neighbor's wife...

10. You shall not covet anything that belongs to your neighbor.

Covet here means to desire what belongs to another. It is considered one of the capital sins in that it is more often than not the source of sin. For teens, to put it more simply, we shouldn't break up other relationships and friendships, whether they are male and male, female and female, or male and female. We shouldn't try to destroy them out of our own need or impoverishment. We should not be so jealous of other people that we have to have exactly what they have in terms of relationships. We should be happy to become ourselves and to develop our own network of friends without always trying to win people to us who may not be so inclined. Basically, this commandment means that we should try to get rid of envy and jealousy in our lives. Of course, feelings of jealousy and envy are something that all human beings have, and we cannot eradicate them completely. But this commandment means that we should recognize these feelings for what they are and learn not to act them out.

JOURNAL EXERCISE

Do Exercise #1, "A Soul-Search: Me and the Ten Commandments," in the Journal, Session 8. Allow group members to share aloud a few of their answers, those they feel comfortable with disclosing to others. Exercise #2, "My Ten Commandments."

DISCUSSION QUESTIONS

1. You have already studied the Beatitudes of the New Testament. Can you see that the Ten Commandments are a more primitive moral code at an earlier stage of Jewish history?

2. Which commandment do you find the most difficult to keep?

SESSION 9: The Sacraments

"Sacraments are 'powers that come forth' from the Body of Christ, which is ever-living and life-giving. They are the actions of the Holy Spirit at work in his Body, the Church. They are the 'masterworks of God' in the new and everlasting Covenant" (CCC# 1116).

The main trouble with the sacraments is that by labeling them we tend to think of them as "things." In reality the word *sacrament* refers to the special "meeting" between Jesus Christ and the person. "The sacraments are efficacious signs instituted by Christ and entrusted to the Church, by which divine life is dispensed to us" (CCC# 1131). There are many ways we can be united to Jesus, of course: by reading his gospel, spending time in prayer, helping the poor and needy, and so on. However, it has always been believed by the Christian community that there is a special encounter between God and persons at significant moments of the human life cycle. Some of these encounters were spoken about by Jesus himself; some were not. It is now the consensus of our community (the Roman Catholic Church) that there are seven of these special moments. Because they are discussed in separate sessions we will not discuss baptism and confirmation here, but move directly to the third sacrament in the Christian initiation process, the Eucharist.

ABOUT SUNDAY MASS OBLIGATION

An issue you may be confronted with in this session is that of the Sunday obligation. Young teenagers often oppose attendance as "meaningless" as a way of testing parental limits. Older youth or young adults sometimes have real doubts or crises of faith which require a lot of dialogue with a helpful adult. Here are three suggestions for dealing with this issue with adolescents:

1. No matter how much you disagree, try to listen patiently to a teenager's objection. Feeling "heard" is half the issue in all probability. In the area of faith we need to show deep respect for another's viewpoint, even if he or she is young.

2. Challenge them and keep them honest. Ask what they contribute to an improved liturgy at the parish. Have they sought out a more meaningful Mass at another time on the weekend than the one they usually attend? Do they choose which Mass to attend based on its time and convenience or on the way that it nourishes their faith?

3. Ask them if they could work on the liturgy with other people their age to render it more meaningful to them. Challenge them to take responsibility in this area.

EUCHARIST

"The Eucharist is the memorial of Christ's Passover, that is, the work of salvation accomplished by the life, death and resurrection of Christ, a work made present in the liturgical action" (CCC# 1409).

This word, *Eucharist*, refers to the most special and intimate union between God and humanity. It is the moment when we literally consume the very person of Jesus Christ under the forms of bread and wine. It's a sacrament instituted by Jesus himself at the Last Supper when he told his apostles to eat his body and drink his blood, for by so doing they would live forever. The Eucharist is "the source and summit of the Christian life" (CCC# 1324).

This sacrament is a very great mystery and beyond our understanding. There's an "old time religion" expression, "Better felt than telt," meaning better experienced than explained, if you want to understand it. So it is with the Eucharist (which we also call "Holy Communion"). By receiving it at Mass we can have a real experience of union with Jesus, and many people who receive the Eucharist regularly can even feel the Lord's presence within them in a spiritual sense. The Eucharist is the greatest gift we could have from God, and it gives us much grace. To "consume" a beloved one is not alien to our psychology. We talk about loving a baby so much we could "eat it up." People who are deeply in love long to be consumed by the other in a spiritual sense, or to be able to break the bonds that isolate us from each other as human beings. And so the idea of consuming Jesus should not strike us as strange, but rather very much in keeping with human psychology.

RECONCILIATION, THE SACRAMENT OF PENANCE
"It is called the 'sacrament of conversion' because it makes us sacramentally present to Jesus' call to conversion, the first step in returning to the Father from whom one has strayed by sin" (CCC #1423).

This is another sacrament that was instituted by Jesus on Easter Sunday when he told his apostles: "Whose sins you shall forgive they are forgiven..." This established the apostles—or today, priests—as representatives in the Christian family of Jesus himself, invested with the power of removing sin in his name.

Today a lot of teenagers criticize this sacrament because they don't understand it. First of all, penance does not excuse us from asking forgiveness of the person we have offended. That is always an important part of reconciliation. "So why do you have to tell your sins to a priest if only God forgives sin?" many young people ask (especially after they've made a real apology). We are not totally sure why Jesus established this practice in the way he did, but we do have some hunches. Maybe it's that Jesus knew human psychology so well that he realized we still often feel guilty even after making an apology. Maybe he knew that the best thing for our security is hearing his official, appointed representative telling us that we are truly and forever forgiven.

This sacrament or special meeting with Jesus should be sought out:

(a) When we have done something seriously wrong;

(b) when there is a sinful pattern developing in our behavior;

(c) when we need to pause and take stock of our Christian life.

This sacrament is also important because it strengthens us with grace to live in a world which often tugs us away from goodness.

MATRIMONY
"The matrimonial covenant, by which a man and a woman establish between themselves a partnership of the whole of life, is by its nature ordered toward the good of the spouses and the procreation and education of offspring; this covenant between the baptized persons has been raised by Christ the Lord to the dignity of a sacrament" (CCC #1601).

Any life choice is a sacred event in that we all have a vocation to fulfill so that we can more and more become our true selves. But the Christian community has given the distinction of sacrament to two of these choices. It has done so with matrimony because it is the way of life chosen by the majority of Christian people. This way of life involves a deep and permanent commitment in love. Being in relationship with another person is a wonderful way to grow into human maturity. We need the experiences of both acceptance and challenge to become the most we can be. And so the Christian community has always looked upon this deep commitment as another special moment with the Lord (or "sacrament").

HOLY ORDERS

"Holy Orders is the sacrament through which the mission entrusted by Christ to his apostles continues to be exercised in the Church until the end of time; thus it is the sacrament of apostolic ministry" (CCC #1536).

Holy Orders refers to ordination to the official priesthood of the church. Priests are leaders in the community as well as in charge of preaching and presiding at the liturgy (Mass) and the celebration of the sacraments. Because ordination is such a special form of service to God and his people, the church considers Holy Orders to be one of the seven sacraments. Those ordained include bishops, priests, and deacons.

ANOINTING OF THE SICK

"By the sacred anointing of the sick and the prayer of the priests the whole Church commends those who are ill to the suffering and glorified Lord, that he may raise them up and save them" (CCC #1499).

Another time in life when we need to have a special moment with the Lord is when we are gravely or chronically ill or near death. This sacrament, which can only be administered by a priest, also gives grace and strength, peace, and the forgiveness of sins for those too ill to confess. Sometimes the grace actually heals the person physically. Sometimes it gives courage to sustain a long illness or chronic condition. Still other times it helps a person to die peacefully. In the gospel we see that very many of the special encounters of Jesus were with people who were seriously ill. The community considers this special form of meeting the Lord a sacrament.

CONCLUSION

Each of the seven sacraments responds to the deep personal need we have of God's redemptive presence at the critical moments of our individual life histories. The sacraments give us "grace," or a life near to God sustained by his strength.

JOURNAL EXERCISE

Do Exercise #1, "The Seven Sacraments" chart in the Journal, and Exercise #2, "Awareness," in the Journal, Session 9.

DISCUSSION QUESTIONS

1. Do you think of Christ more present in the church building than outside of it?

2. What does it mean to say that along with the host we have to "swallow" all of our neighbors? (Louise Evely, *That Man is You*, Westminster, MD: Newman Press, 1965)

A Special Suggestion:

For your closing prayer in this session, have each member of the group kneel in the center of the others who will lay hands on the person's head and shoulders as a sign of Christ's sacramental presence among us. Each individual should be prayed for either silently or aloud (depending on the preference of the group). An example: "Dear Lord, let (first name of teenager) know that you are present in his/her life and care for him/her very deeply."

SESSION 10
PART A
The Apostles' Creed

"Whoever says 'I believe' says 'I pledge myself to what we believe.' Communion in faith needs a common language of faith, normative for all and uniting all in the same confession of faith" (CCC #185).

From the beginning, the early church handed on her faith in a brief formula, especially for candidates for baptism. Called "professions of faith," they are a summary of the faith Christians hold. They are also called "creeds." The "Apostles' Creed" is a summary of the apostles' faith, and we choose it here for its simplicity. Part One of the *Catechism of the Catholic Church* is entitled "The Profession of Faith." It explores in depth the theological meaning behind all of the statements in the Creed. Our suggestion is that you peruse this portion prior to this session. What follows here is a composite of reflections upon the Creed in an attempt to discuss the meaning of its declarations of faith with teenagers.

I believe in God...
It's important at the outset to distinguish the difference between knowing something and believing something. To believe something means accepting without proof. For instance, I believe that this person is trustworthy. I know that this person is six feet tall. That is knowledge of which I am positively assured. And so, when we talk about believing in God, we are not talking about knowing absolutely and certainly. What we are saying is that we have faith, that we trust, that we believe that God exists.

The Father almighty...
God is like a father. God is beyond the masculine and feminine gender. Jesus refers to him as "Abba" or " Father" because he has the characteristics of a good father, not because he is an old man with a white beard. These characteristics would include patience with his children, forgiveness, understanding, generosity, and unconditional love.

Creator of heaven and earth.
This brings us to the question of evolution. There is no conflict between Catholic faith and what you may have learned in school about the theory of evolution. First of all, if we look at the creation of the world, we are told by scientists that probably the earth formed very gradually over billions of years after some initial type of explosion of some particles in the universe. The Bible would tell us that the world was created in seven days. We think today that the Bible account was a poetic way of trying to say that God is the author of the world, that he is the original creator. Today science would tell us that the account in Genesis of the creation makes no sense scientifically. For instance, the sun is created after the light. However this was an attempt, and a good attempt on the part of early believers, to contradict other myths of creation afloat in the pagan world and to say, "No, God is the creator of the world." The main point is that God is the beginner of all things that exist and of all forms of life.

This brings us to the question of the evolution of man and woman. We think too that the story of Adam and Eve is a poetic story to show that God was the creator of the human race. The early Jews did not understand in what scientific way God created man and woman, but they wanted to point out very clearly that they believed that he was the initial creator. And so they gave us the story of Adam and Eve with which you are all familiar.

Adam was created out of the slime of the earth and Eve out the rib of Adam. The very word *Adam* means "Father of the Race." And the word *Eve* means "Mother of the Race." We believe that God created human life as we understand it today. The evolutionist holds the theory that man and woman have evolved from some common ancestor to both the ape and ourselves. It is perfectly acceptable for a Catholic to believe this as long as we also hold that at some point in the evolutionary process God gave man three aspects which do not belong to other creatures in the animal kingdom. Number one: a heart with which to feel, to love and to make free choices. Number two: a highly developed intellect or brain. Number three: the capacity for eternal life forever with God. These three aspects of the human race distinguish us and set us above all of the other creatures.

I believe in Jesus Christ, his only Son, our Lord.

Jesus was the human name given to the baby son of Joseph, the carpenter of Nazareth. *Christ* is a term which was later applied to Jesus, and in Greek means "anointed one" or "divine." To say Jesus Christ means we are saying that we believe that Jesus is both human, as signified by the word *Jesus,* and divine, as signified by the word *Christ*. In other words, he is both man and God at the same time. This is called the doctrine of the incarnation—God into flesh, living among us in the historical person of Jesus.

He was conceived by the power of the Holy Spirit...

This means that Jesus was conceived in a miraculous way in Mary's womb without the benefit of human sexual intercourse. The Christian community has always held, from the earliest times, that Mary was indeed a virgin. Catholic tradition has held and continues to hold Mary to be a very special person in the life of the church.

And born of the Virgin Mary.

There is also the tradition in the Catholic Church that Mary remained a virgin. Now there is some question of an instance in the gospel where it is reported that Jesus' brothers and sisters were outside to see him. However, we know that the same word could be used for "brothers and sisters" as was used for "cousins" in Greek (in which the New Testament was written). There is no clear mention of any brothers and sisters of Jesus, either in the gospel or in tradition. Also, when Jesus was dying on the cross, he entrusted Mary, his mother, to John, his dear friend, and asked John to take care of her. If it was true that he had brothers and sisters, we would presume that this would not have been necessary. And so the community of believers also holds that Mary remained a virgin throughout her life. The community also maintained that Mary was born without original sin. This is called the doctrine of the Immaculate Conception.

He suffered under Pontius Pilate, was crucified, died, and was buried.

It is a mystery why Jesus needed to die in order to save the human race. In the historical order, we can certainly say that he died because he went around preaching things that angered the Jewish and Roman authorities in his day. His preaching was often against conventional wisdom or Jewish beliefs and customs. It took bravery on his part to speak his mind, just as it does for us today to be honest with people. So, because of his honesty in always saying what he really felt and believed, Jesus was crucified by the Roman authorities. This is a good lesson for us about sticking to the truth of our own selves. However, Jesus' crucifixion has a meaning way beyond this.

We know from the book of Genesis in the Bible that the first human beings (Adam and Eve) committed an act of pride and disobedience against God by eating the forbidden fruit. As a result of this "original sin," God stripped the human community of some of its original freedom. Thus we have our present "human condition" which, of course, still includes happiness, but suffering and death as well. The voluntary, selfless crucifixion of Jesus liberates the human race and restores eternal life, that eternal life and freedom which were lost through the original sin of Adam and Eve. Another reality of the crucifixion is that Jesus trusted that his Father would keep him alive, even beyond his physical death, as scary as that death was for him. This is another point for us to bear in mind: Jesus' death should help us to be unafraid of our own death. Just as the Father raised up Jesus after his crucifixion, so too we trust that he will raise us up as well. We call this act of Jesus' death and resurrection our "redemption."

He descended into Hell.

Hell is where "evil doers" will go after this life on earth. "The teaching of the Church affirms the existence of hell and its eternity" (CCC #1035). The chief punishment of hell is separation from God forever, who alone can give us the life of happiness we long for. God does not *plan* for anyone to go to hell; it is the result of a choice of continually turning away from God through mortal sin.

On the third day he rose again.

The reason that Jesus rose was to save us and to demonstrate to all of us that we too will rise, that we too will live forever, that in the Christian life death is overcome. Jesus' rising from the dead is called his "resurrection."

He ascended into heaven...

Forty days after Easter Jesus was no longer apparent to the sight and senses of his disciples. They could in no way see him among them. But after the risen Jesus had appeared to them several times, he took them to a mountain and there departed in a cloud from their midst. This is called the "ascension."

And is seated at the right hand of the Father.

This does not mean so much that Jesus is actually sitting next to his Father. It means that he is no longer present to us in his physical, human form but is only present invisibly by means of the Spirit, and that he is also in heaven, in eternity, just as much as he is present in the world.

He will come again to judge the living and the dead.

Christians believe that faith and good works are necessary for salvation, that it matters how we live our lives. The earlier session we had on the final judgment reminds us that we must live lovingly to attain eternal life with God.

I believe in the Holy Spirit...

The Holy Spirit is Jesus' invisible, continual presence in the world. The Holy Spirit has been symbolized by a dove and by tongues of fire. The Holy Spirit is Jesus' Spirit, still present among us. And so we have in God three "persons" or dimensions: Father, Son, and Spirit. This is called the doctrine of the Trinity—not an intellectual truth to be grasped, but a mystery in which we live our Christian life.

The holy catholic Church...

That's us. We believe that we are God's people, and we believe that all human beings are God's people also. The word *Catholic* means "universal," which includes everybody. But the Roman Catholic Church refers to the community of believers that traces itself all the way back to the apostles and Peter, the first pope. This line of historical (or "apostolic") succession has never been broken.

The communion of saints...

This refers to the bond between the living and the dead. That is to say that in some spiritual way we are linked to those who have died before us and someday we will join them. This is typified in the Catholic Church by the custom of praying to the good people who have died before us whom we call saints. We also pray for "souls in purgatory." Purgatory is an ancient Christian opinion that many good people when they die require some sort of purgation or cleansing before being united to God in heaven.

The forgiveness of sins...

In our session on the sacrament of reconciliation we discussed the significance of the forgiveness of sins. What we must remember is that Jesus, in John 20:19–23, established the way that this forgiveness of sins was concretely to occur in the human community—through the power of absolution he gave to his apostles and their successors.

The resurrection of the body...

This means simply that we will live on after our own death in some recognizable way. Or, to put it in more philosophical terms, that our physical body will be reunited to our soul.

And the life everlasting. Amen.

This means that we believe that life after death is eternal; that it will never end. This is a concept our limited human minds cannot grasp.

JOURNAL EXERCISE

After discussing each line of the Creed with your group, do Exercise #1, "My Creed," in the Journal, Session 10.

DISCUSSION QUESTIONS

1. Does your understanding of the Creed today differ at all from the understanding you had five years ago? How?

2. Is there anything in the Creed which needs more explanation?

PART B
Catholic Identity: Important Definitions

(The following material is also contained in the Journal)

Our identity as Roman Catholic Christians is unique. As mentioned above, we trace ourselves to Peter and the apostles. Our faith is based on God's revelation in scripture, and on tradition that is the practice of the Church community down through the ages. Our identity is also manifested in our religious terminology, and in the doctrinal definitions that reflect our self-understanding. Let's begin with some terms we just discussed in the Creed:

1. Trinity—The mystery of three persons in one God: Father, Son, and Holy Spirit

2. Incarnation—God becoming man in Jesus Christ

3. Redemption—Jesus' saving act for humanity through his death on the cross

4. Resurrection—Jesus being raised from the dead three days after his death on the cross

5. Ascension—Jesus' return to heaven forty days after his resurrection

6. Immaculate Conception—The belief that the Virgin Mary was conceived in her mother's womb without original sin.

7. Assumption—The belief that the Virgin Mary was immediately assumed into heaven after her death

8. Hierarchy—The name given to leadership in the church: the pope, the supreme head of the church, successor to St. Peter; and the bishops who lead the various dioceses throughout the world

9. Liturgy—The official worship of God by the church through the Mass, the sacraments, and other rites of the church as contained in its official books

10. Rosary—A special series of prayers that honor the Virgin Mary as we meditate on the mysteries in her life and in Jesus' life

Other important Roman Catholic definitions:

PRECEPTS OF THE CHURCH

1. Participate in the Sunday Eucharist and refrain from unnecessary work on the Sabbath.

2. Receive Holy Communion during Easter time.

3. Confess serious sins at least once a year.

4. Observe the marriage laws of the church.

5. Help support the church.

6. Do penance, abstaining from meat and fasting from food on the appointed days.

7. Join the missionary spirit and apostolate of the church.

THE CORPORAL WORKS OF MERCY

1. Feed the hungry.

2. Give drink to the thirsty.

3. Clothe the naked.

4. Shelter the homeless.

5. Visit the sick.

6. Visit the imprisoned.

7. Bury the dead.

THE SPIRITUAL WORKS OF MERCY

1. Convert the sinner.

2. Instruct the ignorant.

3. Counsel the doubtful.

4. Comfort the sorrowful.

5. Bear wrongs patiently.

6. Forgive injuries.

7. Pray for the living and the dead.

THE CAPITAL SINS

1. Pride

2. Covetousness

3. Lust

4. Anger

5. Gluttony

6. Envy

7. Sloth

JOURNAL EXERCISE
Do Exercise #2, "My Questions," in the Journal, Session 10

DISCUSSION QUESTIONS

1. While our bond with other Christians is more important than what separates us from them, what is it about being a Roman Catholic that is most special for you?

2. Some of the Capital Sins are English words we do not use very often any more. Can you explain the capital sins in contemporary language?

SESSION 11: The Liturgical Year

Materials needed: A rosary for the Journal exercise

"The Church, in the course of the year...unfolds the whole mystery of Christ from his Incarnation and Nativity through his Ascension, to Pentecost and the expectation of the blessed hope of the coming of the Lord" (CCC #1194).

The liturgical year is made up of two major cycles: *Christmas* (the celebration of Jesus' birth), and *Easter* (the celebration of Jesus' death and resurrection). Each of these major feasts is surrounded by times of preparation and continued celebration. Christmas is prepared for by the season of Advent, and its celebration continues through the feast of the Epiphany. Easter is preceded by the season of Lent. The celebration of Easter is actually three days long, called the "triduum." It begins with the celebration of the Lord's Supper on Holy Thursday, continues with the liturgy of the Passion on Good Friday, and reaches its high point in the Easter Vigil, at which new members of the community are baptized. The celebration of Easter lasts fifty days and includes the feasts of the Ascension and Pentecost. We offer you reflections on two of the seasons of the liturgical year, Advent and Lent.

SOME REFLECTIONS ON ADVENT
(The four weeks preceding Christmas)

Waiting for things is not an American characteristic. All you need do is stand and watch people at a fast-food restaurant to realize this fact. We are used to instant food and drink of all kinds, and instant-on television sets and computers. When you've been on an airplane or a bus that has arrived at its destination, you have witnessed the mad scramble of passengers disembarking. We press forward as if our restlessness and rushing will get us out the door more quickly. We have instant car wash, instant electricity, and jet transportation. This fast-paced world is the only one our teens know. These thoughts are of particular significance during the season of Advent. Advent—the four-week period that the church celebrates to anticipate Christmas—is a reminder that the ancient Jews had to wait for the coming of the Messiah. Advent is meant to stir up within our own hearts a renewed sense of waiting for Jesus. By the power of his Spirit, Jesus is already present among us. Christmas is a time when we celebrate his first coming and gain a deeper sense of his presence in our midst. Advent is the season when the church reminds us that our hearts need careful preparation if Jesus is to come into our lives more fully.

One lesson of Advent, particularly for North Americans, is that most good things take time in coming. Jesus was awaited for almost two thousand years by the Hebrew community. Recall how carefully God chose and formed the little tribe of Abraham into a believing people under great leaders like Moses.

Spiritual growth, like emotional growth, requires a great deal of human experience, plus much time and prayer. Forming relationships, or emotional growth, is a long process. Spiritual growth is also a long process, one that entails fidelity to prayer and worship. The fruit of that fidelity is the coming of Jesus into our lives at an ever deeper level.

Patience does not come easily in the American culture. We speak of rage as a pervasive phenomenon in our culture today. The patient person will often find himself or herself standing alone in a crowd that is rushing about in a frenzy. Those who are patient will often be criticized for their seeming inactivity. And yet, if we are to meet Christ in this closer way we have been speaking about, we have to prepare our hearts quietly, carefully. To expect deep relationship with our Lord immediately is to make the contemporary mistake. Some things can't be hurried. Let us say over and over again to ourselves, "Come, Lord Jesus, come; we are waiting for you."

This session will offer a good opportunity for your young people to reflect on the degree of patience in their own lives. The "patience barometer" is intended to help you begin a discussion of their own thresholds of impatience.

SOME REFLECTIONS ON LENT
(The six weeks preceding Easter)

Lent is the penitential season in the church calendar when we reflect on the mystery of Jesus' suffering and death. Since ancient times, Christians have undertaken penitential practices such as fasting and abstaining from meat. In our pleasure-oriented culture today, there is little attention given to penance or asceticism.

Asceticism is a harsh-sounding word. It comes from a Greek word meaning "to exercise." It refers not to prayer itself but to our preparation for prayer—serious prayer. Asceticism and penance are never ends in themselves. They are means to a more spiritual life, a deeper union with God. Asceticism implies that we have the self-discipline to pray for whatever amount of time we have promised ourselves we would, no matter how many distractions come our way.

In a more remote sense, diet and physical exercise are ascetical practices related to prayer. Prayer time needs to be removed from normal time and party time. The more balanced and nutritious our diet, the better the tone our bodies will have, and the more we will feel prepared to turn to prayer. So too with exercise. Exercise tones our bodies and clears our minds so that we are more easily able to turn to God in prayer. Another form of asceticism, perhaps the most necessary today, is the patience and slowing down we talked about in the season of Advent. Discuss with your group whether or not they feel that self-imposed penance can be helpful.

Last, here is a list of "holy days" that punctuate the liturgical calendar. Catholics keep these days sacred by attending Mass:

HOLY DAYS OF OBLIGATION IN THE UNITED STATES
1. Solemnity of Mary, Mother of God (January 1)

2. Ascension Thursday (forty days after Easter)

3. Assumption of Mary (August 15)

4. All Saints' Day (November 1)

5. Immaculate Conception (December 8)

6. Christmas (December 25)

JOURNAL EXERCISE

Review the seasons of the church year. Then do Exercise #1, "My Patience Barometer," and Exercise #2, "A Practical Promise," in the Journal, Session 11.

DISCUSSION QUESTIONS

1. Which is your favorite liturgical season? Why?

2. Is Christmas more of a material or spiritual celebration for you?

Note: At the end of this session in the Journal is a description of four popular Catholic devotions. While not a part of the liturgy, they are common ways that Catholics have prayed down through the ages. Review these with your group.

I Have Chosen You: Test

(This test may be copied)

Date_____ Name _____

A. The fourth, sixth, and ninth commandments are:

1. (4th) _____

2. (6th) _____

3. (9th) _____

4. The meaning of the first commandment for us today is: _____

5. What is one way, besides a physical act, to break the fifth commandment? _____

B. What are the seven sacraments and the corresponding symbolism?

Sacrament	Symbolism
6. _____	13. _____
7. _____	14. _____
8. _____	15. _____
9. _____	16. _____
10. _____	17. _____
11. _____	18. _____
12. _____	19. _____

20. Any Christian can administer the sacrament of baptism.

   Is this statement true or false? _____

C. Some important terms: _____

21. God becoming man is the_____

22. Jesus being raised from the dead is _____

23. That Mary was conceived without sin is the _____

24. The official worship of the church is the _____

25. The leadership of the church is the _____

D. Five of the six precepts of the church are

26. _____

27. _____

28. _____

29. _____

30. _____

E. The four major cycles of the church are

31. _____

32. _____

33. _____

34. _____

35. The assumption of the Blessed Virgin Mary is celebrated each year on (month)_____, (day)_____.

36. The holy day we celebrate on November 1 is _____

F. Write the Apostles' Creed (fourteen lines, fourteen points):

(Each answer [except for F., the Creed] is worth two points)   Final Grade _____

Session 12: Community Service Project

Confirmation programs today ordinarily require service on the part of candidates. This flows from our understanding of "catechesis" as including "leading to service." Many parishes have successfully initiated these programs and others have had difficulty. If your parish has been successful in this area, then retain what has worked in the past. However, difficulties can arise for one or more of the following reasons:

1. The service project is viewed as "one more hurdle" to the reception of confirmation on the part of parents and/or candidates.

2. The individual service is difficult for a Director of Religious Education (D.R.E.) or volunteer catechist to monitor.

3. The nature of suitable service is difficult to define. For example, is walking the neighbor's dog really service?

4. Volunteer work at many human service agencies may provide no involvement with people—just clerical work or some form of manual labor.

5. The demands of a teenager's time by other school and social activities is excessive.

Because we feel that we wish to leave young people with a positive experience of service, and because in our realism we recognize that this sacramental preparation process is probably being led by parish volunteers, we suggest the following:

1. That the entire group plus the leader (and perhaps some parents and/or sponsors) do the project together as a community.

2. That the service, in the wider community, be a new cultural exposure for the youth—something to which he or she is not usually exposed.

3. That there be time set aside for group reflection on the experience (using the "Community Service Project" reflection sheet for session 12 in the Journal).

4. That if individuals in the group as a result of this exposure wish to continue in service, this enthusiasm be supported by the adult leader.

Suggested examples of a service project:

1. serving lunch in a soup kitchen

2. spending an afternoon with low -income children in a day care facility

3. visiting a nursing home

4. visiting a home for mentally challenged

5. visiting chronic patients in a veteran's hospital, or hospice, or home for people living with HIV/AIDS

6. doing some specific manual labor project for a poor person or family (e.g., painting the house) whom the young people also meet

7. visiting a children's hospital

8. visiting individual parish shut-ins

9. affluent suburban Catholic youth doing a joint activity with Catholic urban youth from the inner city

10. visiting a Catholic Worker house

JOURNAL EXERCISE

Do "Community Service Project" reflection sheet in the Journal, Session 12.

SESSION 13: Parent/Youth "Mini" Retreat

Time: 1 hour, 45 minutes

Theme: The Gifts of the Holy Spirit

According to the revised code of canon law, parents are not to be sponsors of their children at confirmation. There is wisdom in the church's recognition that it is helpful for young people to have "that special adult"— someone to assist them in their spiritual journey. Teenagers sometimes have difficulty in confiding in parents at this stage and yet still need adult guidance. On the other hand, parents and guardians have been the most significant people in the faith development of their children to this point. They were probably responsible for their baptism; it is fitting that they are brought into the continuance of the initiation process. The "Rite of Choice" and today's retreat are two ways we include parents in this process. They will also be asked to write a letter to their teenager on the "Christian Story" Retreat.

WELCOME
(5 minutes)

The D.R.E. or leader welcomes everyone. He or she announces that the theme of the day is the "Gifts of the Holy Spirit." These seven gifts dispose us to God's inspiration and help us to live holier lives. They should be written on a board or poster paper: (1) wisdom, (2) understanding, (3) right judgment, (4) courage, (5) knowledge, (6) reverence, (7) fear (awe) of the Lord.

Invite participants to share today as much as possible so that we may all grow in the Spirit.

TALK #1
(15 minutes)

(By a teenager or young adult already confirmed.) This talk focuses on the gifts of the Spirit, particularly the first four. The speaker discusses how he or she needs wisdom, understanding, right judgment, and courage in life, including for the relationship with his or her parent(s). Personal examples of difficulties in relating to parents, plus a discussion of growth in those areas, are crucial to the talk, that should conclude with a discussion of God's Spirit in his or her life.

DISCUSSION GROUPS
(30 minutes)

Divide people into groups of eight. Separate parents and teens, putting four of each per group. Also try to separate spouses in assigning groups. Each group member needs a pencil to complete the index card he or she receives. Four of the gifts are focused on in this exercise. Give one card of the four different gifts to each parent group member and one card of the four gifts to each teenager. All are instructed to write a sentence stating how they need the gift more in their life as they try to relate to their teen or parent. One teen and one parent will be talking about each of the four gifts.

(One of each card to a teenager and an adult in every group)

WISDOM		UNDERSTANDING
RIGHT JUDGMENT		COURAGE

The leader should assign someone to initiate discussion in each group after the cards have been completed.

COFFEE BREAK
(15 minutes)

TALK #2
(15 minutes)

(Talk should be given by a parent. It would be better if he or she were not a member of today's group.) The topic is the same as Talk #1, except that it is a parent's perspective on trying to relate to his or her teenager.

CLOSING
PRAYER CIRCLE
(25 minutes)

Invite everyone to sit in a circle. Light a candle in the center and dim the lights. Play a recorded song about the Holy Spirit, or one that has some theme relating to this retreat.

Reading #1:
"On Children," from *The Prophet* by Kahlil Gibran (New York: Knopf, 1982).

> And a woman who held a babe against
> her bosom said, Speak to us of Children.
> And he said:
> Your children are not your children.
>
> They are the sons and daughters of Life's
> longing for itself.
> They come through you but not from you,
> and though they are with you yet they belong
> not to you.
>
> You may give them your love but not your
> thoughts,
> for they have their own thoughts.
> You may house their bodies but not their souls,
> for their souls dwell in the house of tomorrow,
> which you cannot visit, not even in your
> dreams.

You may strive to be like them, but seek
not to make them like you.
For life goes not backward nor tarries
with yesterday.

You are the bows from which your children
as living arrows are sent forth.
The archer sees the mark upon the path of the
infinite, and He bends you with His might
that His arrows may go swift and far.
Let your bending in the archer's hand be for
gladness;
for even as He loves the arrow that flies,
so He loves also the bow that is stable.

Reading #2:

**If I speak in the tongues of mortals and of angels, but do not have love, I am a noisy gong
or a clanging cymbal. And if I have prophetic powers, and understand all mysteries and
all knowledge, and if I have all faith, so as to remove mountains, but do not have love, I
am nothing. If I give away all my possessions, and if I hand over my body so that I may
boast, but do not have love, I gain nothing.**

**Love is patient; love is kind; love is not envious or boastful or arrogant or rude. It
does not insist on its own way; it is not irritable or resentful; it does not rejoice in wrongdoing, but rejoices in the truth. It bears all things, believes all things, hopes all things,
endures all things. (1 Corinthians 13:1–7)**

Invite people to pray silently or spontaneously. After ten minutes or so invite everyone to join hands and pray
the Lord's Prayer for an increase of gifts of the Holy Spirit.

SESSION 14: Self-Acceptance

"God who created man out of love also calls him to love—the fundamental and innate vocation of every human being. For man is created in the image and likeness of God who is himself love" (CCC #1604).

In his treatise on the love of God, St. Bernard of Clairvaux tells us that the first step in the love of God is to love oneself. How true this is! If I don't feel lovable it will be very difficult to feel loved by anyone else, or by God. This problem of low self-esteem is a serious issue for many teenagers. In his book, *The Five Cries of Youth: Issues That Trouble Young People Today* (New York: Harper Collins, 1993), which surveyed thousands of teenagers, Merton Strommen and Ram Gupta report that self-hatred is a major problem for many, many young people. Symptoms of this are problems with peer relationships, academic problems, dating problems, eating disorders, alcohol and drug abuse, and aggressive behavior. It's not too difficult to spot a teenager with low self-esteem. For many young people their chief issue in life is just dealing with their sense of self. When this is the case, your role as a leader is simply to provide them with warmth and acceptance. If you convey a positive attitude toward them their own self-love will slowly grow along with their ability to trust. You might say this is not too "spiritual," or that it seems more of a psychological issue. That's because some of us grew up in an era that compartmentalized human beings into their physical, emotional, and spiritual selves. Now we are realizing that we just can't chop ourselves up like that. Our spiritual and psychological selves are so intertwined that growth in one of those areas is also growth in the other. To the teenager with low self-esteem for whom we provide affirmation, we are God's emissary, the representative of his love and his acceptance of them. In a document written to provide guidance for us in youth ministry in the church, "A Vision of Youth Ministry" (ibid.,) the authors state that two of the fundamental principles are:

1. Youth ministry is concerned with the total person.

2. Youth ministry involves, first and foremost, not programs, but relationships.

James Fowler, in his book *Stages of Faith: the Psychology of Human Development* (San Francisco: Harper, 1995), has done a lot of research in the area of the stages of faith we go through as we mature throughout life. Using the term *synthetic conventional* for stage three of faith development, Fowler feels that most adolescents fall within this category between ages twelve and eighteen. The most distinctive characteristic of this stage is a concern with the interpersonal—which of course indicates that spirituality for adolescents is basically in interpersonal terms. Adults who minister with youth at this stage need to be genuine, sincere, warm, and open. At this stage young people can begin to relate to Jesus Christ as a friend and companion. In former times people who wanted to be closer to God were taught to be self-deprecating. A sample of this approach is the following from a fifteenth century book, *The Imitation of Christ*, by Thomas à Kempis:

> But if I humble myself and acknowledge my
> own nothingness, and cast away all manner of
> esteem of myself and (as I really am) account myself
> to be mere dust, your grace will be favorable to me
> and your light will draw near to my heart. (Book III, Chapter 8)

While *The Imitation of Christ* has many good points, the book is not recommended for young people today. Since the days of Thomas à Kempis we have developed better ways of understanding our relationship with God.

Thomas à Kempis was on target when he said that a "swelled head," or feelings of superiority, interfere with spiritual growth. But he was only getting at a defense mechanism, not at the root of the problem. The real issue is that, deep down, people who have an inflated ego really don't think they are worth anything at all. They usually pick one aspect of themselves—their good looks, their skill in some sport, or their brains—then use that one thing to try to get people to like them or look up to them. If they really felt good and secure about themselves they wouldn't have to brag. Neither would they have to lash out or be violent in threats or even in actions. Low self-esteem is further exacerbated by bullying. The young person who is bullied by peers suffers continuous emotional blows. Sadly, in our country the extreme results of bullying in school are shootings and other violent episodes.

There are many things teenagers do to hide their low self-esteem. These things are called defense mechanisms. One defense is shyness. Another defense is to act very aloof and independent. Sticking with just one close friend and constantly putting others down are also ways of dealing with personal inferiority. Still another is to be involved in using drugs: alcohol, marijuana, "designer drugs," and even cocaine and heroin. During their "Christian Story" retreat, your group will have the opportunity to explore their own defense mechanisms. But perhaps you could initiate them to think about this issue now. Studies have shown that self-esteem rises after people leave high school. This is because after high school, young persons can choose how to define themselves, whereas when they are still in school their peers provide a large measuring stick. This session provides a chance for group members to talk about pressures they feel to conform in a negative way. What keeps them from being who they truly are?

Love is the theological virtue that causes us to love God above all things and to love our neighbor, for the sake of God, as we love ourselves. Self-love sometimes means selfishness that pulls us away from God and neighbor. But a healthy self-image means that we respect our goodness because we were created by God and because we are the object of his love. As the Jewish philosopher, Hillel, put it: "If I am not for myself, who will be? If I am only for myself, what will I become?"

JOURNAL EXERCISE
Do Exercise #1, "A Self-Image Inventory," and Exercise #2, "Windows to Myself," in the Journal, Session 14.

DISCUSSION QUESTIONS
1. How do you think you got your self-image?

3. Do you feel responsible to work on your own self-esteem?

SESSION 15: Community

"In the primitive community of Jerusalem, the disciples 'devoted themselves to the apostle's teaching and fellowship, to the breaking of bread and the prayers'" (CCC #949).

Community is at the very heart of our faith. St. John says that God is love and those who abide in love abide in God, and God abides in them (1 John: 4:16). This "abiding in love" is commonly known as *community*. The English word *love* is used for a variety of meanings. But *love*, in the Christian sense, is called *agape* in the New Testament. St. Paul uses this word to speak of the mutual love among the faithful believers. Agape for him is a kind of atmosphere in which God and Christians live together. It is rooted in our mutual baptism. Because of that reality we are united both to God and to one another as members of God's family.

Sometimes teenagers use the word *love* only to describe a romantic attraction. It can also be limited to denote the relationship with one's human family or close friends. But what young people need to try to begin to understand is that we are all a part of the human community and that all baptized persons are members of the Christian community. This does not mean that we need to like everybody, agree with everybody, and feel emotionally attracted to everybody. What it does mean is that we need to try to respect each and every person as God's child and our brother and sister. We need to be patient with each other, work toward mutual understanding, and support each other in our struggles on life's journey. This is how Jesus wanted his followers to behave. Hopefully your parish, and certainly this group, are a microcosm of the larger Christian community. We need to draw into our circle those who feel marginalized, forgotten, judged, and rejected.

James Gilligan, M.D., in his book, *Violence: Reflections on a National Epidemic* (New York: Putnam, 1996), offers excellent insights on the roots of violence in our society. Young people who fail to build reserves of self-love suffer from the deficiency which Gilligan labels "shame." Shame is the opposite of a healthy pride in oneself. He writes that the "purpose of violence is to diminish the intensity of shame" (p. 111). "Violence is an attempt to restore justice by replacing shame with pride" (p. 185). "The best way to prevent someone from laughing at you is to make them cry instead..." (p. 184). It is deep feelings of inferiority that have been the root cause of murders by young people. At times the most trivial of acts, like being given a "dirty" look, called a demeaning name, or having one's sneakers stepped on, have resulted in acts of lethal violence.

The need to belong to a caring, accepting group is real. This is what membership in youth gangs is all about: the feeling of being a part of something, of belonging. But what happens when the group does not accept a certain young person? The crowd can work either as an enabler or as a destroyer. While the former enables the young person to achieve an identity, the latter destroys all remaining feelings of worth and self-esteem. As anyone who has observed the patterns of adolescent growth knows, young people can be brutally cruel. If a particular individual doesn't have the necessary tribal traits—good looks, an outgoing personality, lots of dates, exceptional marks, athletic ability, or whatever—he or she can be locked out of the group in merciless fashion. As mentioned previously, these young people may even be the victims of bullying. This is where the church comes in. As a caring, accepting group which is open to all at any time, the church can offer a setting for all young people. What we need to do is make sure that our parish is not just an "adult" church. Young people need to be involved. They should be serving as lectors and in other forms of ministry—as choir members, members of parish committees, and so on. This will be even more true after their confirmation. One excellent way parishes can offer to challenge youth is to invite them into a formalized peer ministry program. It is crucial that youth as youth feel themselves to be vital, significant members of their parish community.

The Christian community finds its fullest expression when God's people assemble to celebrate a eucharistic liturgy. Also what are traditionally called the four "marks" of the church exemplify the Catholic community: the church is (1) *one*, or has unity, (2) *holy*, (3) *catholic*, embracing everyone, and (4) *apostolic*, tracing itself back to St. Peter and the early Christian community.

JOURNAL EXERCISE

Do Exercise # 1, "My 'Love' Report Card," in the Journal, and Exercise #2, "Anger Inventory," Session 15.

DISCUSSION QUESTIONS

1. Do you feel apart from, or a part of your parish when you attend Sunday Mass?

2. Do you feel a sense of belonging with any group of which you are a member?

Note: This session provides an opportunity to celebrate being a community by either having refreshments in your meeting place or going out to eat together as a group.

SESSION 16
PART A
Ministry

"In all of his life Jesus presents himself as our model. He is the perfect man, who invites us to become his disciples and follow him" (CCC #520).

Ministry or service is a translation of the Greek word *diakonia* that appears in a passage from the Acts of the Apostles. "Ordained" ministry refers to the sacrament of Holy Orders or sacramental priesthood, but all Christians, including teenagers, are called to ministry. It is Jesus Christ who is our model in ministry, the man who taught us by his life and word that happiness is never found in selfish self-seeking. Deep joy is found in service to others. Jesus most clearly symbolizes how we should live when he washes his apostles' feet before the Last Supper and tells us that we must "wash the feet" of one another. You, as a catechist or leader of youth, are right now ministering by teaching, building community, and leading young people into prayer and service.

Being a minister means never saying that we are better or more advanced than anyone else. It never means that we don't have as much to gain as to give when we minister to another person.

> Ministry means the ongoing attempt to put one's own search for God, with all the moments of pain and joy, despair and hope, at the disposal of those who want to join this search but do not know how....We lay down our life to give new life....We realize that young people call for Christians who are willing to develop their sensitivity to God's presence in their own lives, as well as the lives of others, and to offer their experience as a way of recognition and liberation to their fellow people. (Henri Nouwen, *Creative Ministry*. New York: Doubleday, 1971, p. 116)

As adults we must be very careful to remember that our age may give us some wisdom but not "position" over and above young people. They are, in a sense, "teachers" to us as we are to them. (But you already realize this by now!)

Maria Harris, in her book *Portrait of Youth Ministry* (New York/Ramsey: Paulist Press, 1981), discusses *diakonia* as *troublemaking*. She means that word in this sense. If service calls us to the spiritual and corporal works of mercy, from feeding the hungry to visiting the sick, in today's complex world this necessarily involves institutions. Our challenge as Christian ministers is to challenge or "cause trouble" for institutions which are unjust, oppress people, foster poverty, and degrade the human being.

Another way to discuss ministry is in terms of peer to peer relationships among teenagers. Erik Erikson, the famous psychologist, wrote in the introduction to his book, *Identity, Youth and Crisis* (New York: Norton, 1968): "Thus the relative waning of the parents and the emergence of the young adult specialist as the permanent and permanently changing authority is bringing about a shift by which older youth guided by such young authority will have to take increasing responsibility for the orientation of the specialists and of older youth. This, however, we can only do by recognizing and cultivating an age-specific ethical capacity in older youth, which is the true criterion of identity." Research in moral development, has concluded that social interaction with one's peers whose moral ideas and ideals are slightly ahead of one's own conceptual development, stimulates both cognitive and moral growth.

Involving older teenagers and young adults as speakers and group leaders on the retreat weekend this year will demonstrate the power of peers ministering to peers. Many public high schools employ peer helping programs in their guidance department. S.A.D.D. (Students Against Driving Drunk) is an excellent example of peer:peer service.

Examples of peer ministry are also abounding in adult life. Take the young couple who find the romantic gilded edge that first surrounded their relationship fast fading and a new sharpened focus on the faults and irritating habits of each other invading their marital bliss. It would be far more helpful for such a couple to seek advice from friends who have been married only a few years longer than they have, and in whose memory this "crisis" is still fresh, than it would be to go to a sage elderly couple who have so assimilated the experience of accepting each other's faults that it has faded in the margins of memory. Another example would be a person young in the spiritual life who is experiencing aridity in prayer for the first time. Someone only a few months or years beyond this experience can often be of more practical help than a person well-advanced in the spiritual life. There is no need to multiply examples to emphasize this point. To summarize this brief discussion let us say that as parents and teachers wane, in one sense, as models during the onset of adolescence, peers are the most potentially effective stimulators of moral, spiritual, and even psychological growth.

As for the "benefits" or spiritual rewards of ministry for the young person, Merton Strommen has also done research in this area. He found that for youth in peer: peer ministry:

1. Self-esteem increased dramatically, and self-criticism and personal anxiety decreased.

2. The youth increased measurably in their openness to people.

3. Anxiety decreased and openness to others was enhanced.

This can be summed up in the words of Jack, age seventeen, who remarked after a week of work on a volunteer project with poor people in Appalachia: "I got more out of this week than I gave. It makes me feel better about myself."

We spoke earlier about the Beatitudes where Jesus says that blessed are...those who, in summary, serve the needs of others. Yes, their rewards will be rich in heaven, but they are also happy here and now. Merton Strommen and young Jack are saying in psychological terms what Jesus is telling us in the gospel: that his gift to us is peace if we lay down our lives for others.

JOURNAL EXERCISE
Do Exercise #1, "Ministry Mirror," in the Journal, Session 16.

DISCUSSION QUESTIONS:
1. *Compassion* is a word which literally means "to suffer with"; how does this word relate to ministry?

2. What gift do you feel God has given you to minister to other people?

PART B
Social Justice

As our world shrinks, media expands, and the Internet links us around the globe, we have become increasingly aware of the injustice in our world, the struggles of the developing world, and the presence of violence, terrorism, and war. Our bishops in the United States have assumed leadership in trying to help us understand the connection between world conditions and the gospel. In their pastoral letter, "This Land Is Home To Me," the bishops of Appalachia stated: "Action on behalf of justice is a constitutive element of preaching the Gospel."

As we have discussed, the teen years are supposed to be a time for discovering oneself, working out what is called "identity," and seeing oneself as an individual with unique qualities. But there is a danger in this type of self-preoccupation. A person can become so absorbed in self that his or her vision is extremely narrowed. When that takes place the person's view of life doesn't correspond to the truth. It is too constricted a vision. Jesus has given us an antidote for this excessive introspection. It is a clear and unmistakable mandate to care for the poor of this world. The gospels present Jesus as preferentially associating with the poor and others on the fringes of society—lepers, sick people, those possessed, prostitutes, and all others left out or rejected by society for one reason or another.

Living in a rich nation, surrounded by affluence, constantly badgered to take up a consumer-oriented, selfish way of life—all these pressures can shape an individual into something less than a complete and willing follower of Christ. It would not be surprising if such a person developed blind spots when certain strong gospel statements showed up. How could one take the words of Christ literally and still continue to live with a "me first" attitude toward life? Today we see that it is not just enough to act justly on an individual level; we need to be concerned with the institutions of society as well. For example, in the early days of our country slavery was a very common practice in the South. Many slaves were Christians and many slave masters were also Christians. Slavery to many of them seemed very appropriate as long as the slaves were treated kindly. Of course today we look back and say that that society was caught in a sinful structure without perhaps being too aware of it. We say "sinful" because the very idea of slavery goes against one of the basic tenets of Jesus Christ: that we are all equals in God's eyes. This equality and dignity which each person deserves is called "justice." And so we would say that any structure which is unjust is sinful or morally wrong, and slavery is a structure which places people as in superior and inferior positions.

Another sinful structure is racism. Racism says that the color of one's skin determines who is superior and who is inferior in our society. Yet another is sexism, that contends that either males or females are superior to the opposite sex. Other sinful structures are any that put down minority groups based on such things as their nationality, their religion, their sexual orientation, and so forth. And so it is that when we examine our consciences to see if we have also sinned, or refused to love in our personal lives, we also need to ask ourselves if we are a part of any sinful structures in our society.

JOURNAL EXERCISE
Do Exercise #2, "Peace and Justice Questionnaire," in the Journal, Session 16.

SESSION 17: Morality

"The doctrine of original sin, closely connected with that of redemption by Christ, provides lucid discernment of man's situation in the world....Ignorance of the fact that man has a wounded nature inclined to evil gives rise to serious errors in the areas of education, politics, social action and morals" (CCC #407).

Morality is a word that is often misunderstood. Many people see the word as synonymous with sexual behavior—immoral referring to inappropriate or wrong sexual behavior. Still other people understand the word *moral* to refer to honesty in business dealings. Both of these interpretations are very limited in scope. They have probably developed for cultural reasons, and perhaps newer words are needed to express a broader range of right and wrong behavior. Moral and immoral refer to inner attitudes as well as to external behavior. The feeling of love in our hearts, or the intellectual idea of love, is not enough. Love must be translated from feeling and thinking into concrete action in order to be real and credible. Loving is not only an interior disposition, it is action with and for others. It is precisely this action which is the living out of Christianity and following Jesus Christ's way of life. Some popular songs have lyrics about the nature of love. But if the ideas of love remain within us like the lyrics of a song and never get translated into action, then the words of love are empty and meaningless. **If a brother or sister is naked and lacks daily food, and one of you says to them, "Go in peace; keep warm and eat your fill," and yet you do not supply their bodily needs, what is the good of that? So faith by itself, if it has no works, is dead** (James 2:15–17).

Conscience

"Conscience is a judgment of reason whereby the human person recognizes the moral quality of a concrete act that he is going to perform, is in the process of performing, or has already completed" (CCC #1778).

Action and behavior are the proof of loving, beyond words and thoughts and feelings. A person can be said to live a moral life if he or she is really trying to put love (and all that the word encompasses) into practice. Immorality is basically a refusal to care about others; it is selfishness. It can take the form of sexual behavior or dishonesty in business dealings, but it has a thousand other faces. Failure to share one's material goods or failure to communicate within the family is also immoral.

This brings us to a discussion of conscience. Conscience, some of us were taught, is the little voice within us pointing out right from wrong. Guilt is its by-product when we have chosen a wrong attitude or action. As we mature, our understanding of conscience needs to mature. A more adult way to understand this psychological/spiritual dimension of our personalities is to think of conscience as a developed sensitivity or a willing awareness. It means that we keep ourselves open and allow the message of love in the gospel to flood our entire being. It means that we keep before our mind's eye the command of Jesus to love our neighbor as ourselves. We choose not to block this commandment from our conscious awareness so as to develop a mature Christian conscience. We allow the needs of others to affect us. Conscience is to be distinguished from "scrupulosity," a minute critical examination of all our actions that, in the end, blocks all action. A mature Christian conscience is one that tries to see the world with the eyes of Jesus Christ, and tries to keep alive within us an attitude of compassion and gentleness. This is what it means to live a moral life.

To "form" our consciences in order to make moral choices, we need to undergo a process of reflection:

1. Consider the viewpoint of Catholicism: (a) The Ten Commandments, (b) Jesus' teaching in the gospel, and (c) the church's teachings (its traditions as well as present-day teachings of the pope and bishops).

2. Discuss matters with people who can help us be objective (not young people only, but also those with more life experience).

3. Pray to the Lord about our choices.

4. Listen to our heart's honest feelings.

5. Make a decision and stick to it.

In this session, try to help your young people become more reflective concerning the choices they make every day.

Sin

We can summarize morality as loving behavior. To relate the word *sin* to this approach to morality, we can go back to the original Greek meaning of the verb "to sin" which is "to miss the mark." This translation might throw a whole new light on the word. As a child you probably had an idea of sin as a bad action or black mark on your soul, or even something associated with purity, sexuality, or unclean language. But as in so many other aspects of religion, there is a more mature understanding of sin.

To "miss the mark" can also be said in this way: not to be your best self. When we look at sin in this general way we can equate it with our discussion of moral behavior. To love is a constant struggle, and many times we fail to act in the most loving way because of our own laziness or selfishness or weakness. We miss the mark of doing the loving thing; we fail to be the best self we can be. In no way does this approach to sin minimize our wrongdoing. But what it does do is to keep the focus on our behavior and our struggle to be good people. It doesn't say that since we have sinned we are evil people; so a good self-image is compatible with the daily struggle to grow and love in spite of the fact that we fail so often.

Mortal and Venial Sin

Sin is such an abstract reality that it is impossible to categorize. And yet, for the sake of understanding the meaning of a moral life, we have to distinguish among sins. "The root of all sin lies in man's heart" (CCC #1873). The Catechism talks about mortal (serious) sin and venial (not as serious) sin: "For a sin to be mortal, three conditions must together be met: Mortal sin is sin whose object is grave matter and which is also committed with full knowledge and deliberate consent" (CCC #1857). It is the heart that must be searched to know the degree of sinfulness. Theologians today talk about sin not so much as a specific act but as the "drift" or patterns of a person's life. For example, a husband who neglects his relationship with his wife over a long period of time, who fails to communicate and share with her, may eventually become involved with another woman (adultery). And so it is the drift that this man's life has taken away from his wife which is a sin in addition to any sexual act. Mortal or serious sin is when the wrong pattern does become so much a part of a person's life that it affects the entire being and turns it away from God.

Guilt

Guilt is the product of our conscience; it flows from our sensitivity to our failures. Guilt is often characterized by a depressed feeling, a feeling which carries a dislike for our sinfulness and sometimes even an intense dislike for ourselves.

The first thing we need to understand about guilt is that feelings have no morality; they are neither good nor bad. Sexual feelings, angry feelings, fed-up feelings are not wrong to have. The right or wrong comes in the way we express our feelings, because sometimes we express them inappropriately. But the feelings themselves should not give us a sense of guilt. Another thing that should not arouse guilt is the appropriate expression of anger. Anger is a healthy emotion, and if it is buried inside it can do serious damage. Justified anger may be expressed verbally, or we can admit it to ourselves and choose not to express it.

If we sin and act in an unloving manner, it is healthy to feel guilt, shame, remorse, irritation with ourselves. Out of these feelings can come resolutions to change or repair our behavior, and also to continue the struggle for holiness. This is healthy guilt; unhealthy guilt lets us wallow in our emotions, feel self-hatred, get depressed. We indulge these feelings as a substitute for making concrete resolutions and taking steps to change our behavior. Thus we say that guilt is useful—but it should lead to action.

Sexuality

The strong emergence of sexual feelings and the ensuing confusion is part of what we all remember about being a teenager. It is difficult for youth today to live out Christian values in the sexual area because there is little support for that in the culture at large. Various studies are alarming in terms of the number of teenagers, even very young teenagers, reporting sexual activity. Teenage pregnancy continues to rise. Also we are aware that some of our youth may have a homosexual orientation, or may fear that they do. If a teenager brings up a sexual question, issue, or problem with you, consider that you are trusted. It's probably the riskiest area a teenager could discuss with an adult. Despite their seeming sophistication, young people often still harbor many questions and fears in the area of sexuality. The following are a few suggestions for addressing sexual issues with teens.

1. Try to remain calm, unshocked, and open if they begin to discuss sex. They are asking for help, so ask some questions which probe a bit if seemingly they are having difficulty saying what they want to say. (Being comfortable with your own sexuality is of course the best preparation for a conversation of this nature.)

2. Be accepting of them. It is important to help them make a distinction between a bad act or choice and being a bad person.

3. While being accepting of them as a person, don't be afraid to be firm in upholding the cherished Catholic viewpoint that sexual intercourse should be reserved to marriage where commitment to the other and to an offspring can be protected. Young people need this guidance badly. Even

though there is so much societal pressure on them to engage in sex, they are often very uncomfortable about it.

4. Try to be aware of what Charles Shelton, S.J. calls "developmental limitedness" in his book *Adolescent Spirituality* (Chicago: Loyola University Press, 1983). That is to say, you need to have a "pastoral realism" about teenage sexuality and at the same time challenge them to further spiritual growth and responsibility.

5. Try to help them realize that the church has accumulated a real wisdom down through the centuries and is not opposed to every pleasure in life, but rather is concerned about the deep-down, inner peace of its members—the kind of happiness Jesus talks about. The church knows, and thus teaches, that when a person doesn't have the emotional maturity to commit himself or herself totally and forever to another, sexual involvement will eventually cause stress and suffering. It will be too much for an adolescent to deal with. Also, the prospect of a baby is not fair to the child and can be a great source of stress for a teenage parent.

By focusing on sexuality we are not implying that there are not many other significant moral issues today. The church is disapproving of capital punishment, abortion, and birth control. There are serious bioethical issues like cloning and embryonic research raised by our advanced medical technology. We do not have time to explore all these here, but hopefully a confirmed Christian will be exploring these issues from the church's perspective as he or she matures in the faith.

Morality is a term applied to human conduct. It is a norm which determines whether human actions are right and fitting or bad and unbefitting a follower of Jesus Christ. Moral acts must be considered within the context of their circumstances and their ends. The pope and bishops provide guidance for the church in matters of morals.

JOURNAL EXERCISE
Do Exercise #1, "My Morality," and Exercise #2, "Friends: My 'Moral' Mirror," in the Journal, Session 17.

DISCUSSION QUESTIONS
1. Do you feel pressure to "follow the crowd?" Give examples.

2. How do you cope when you feel pressured by peers in the area of alcohol and other drugs?

PERIOD OF PURIFICATION AND ENLIGHTENMENT

At this point we are moving closer to the season of Lent and the final phase of this sacramental preparation process. The retreat will soon be completed. If there is a young person who is still hostile to being confirmed, this would be an appropriate point at which he or she should withdraw from the process after discussion with the confirmation director, parish priest, and parents. To withdraw at this stage could help to preserve the faith of a rebellious or negative teenager. Forcing such teenagers to continue could ultimately alienate them further from the institution of the church. Dioceses generally have a special adult confirmation preparation program, or perhaps the young person will be ready to make that commitment the following year. **Confirmation does not at all need to correspond to a particular grade level in school!**

The entire church community moves into a period of purification as these young people move into the final phase of their confirmation preparation. This period begins with the "Rite of Enrollment" in which the candidates formally enroll their names and the parish community gives its approval for them to be confirmed into the fullness of the Christian community. While we place the "Christian Story" Retreat as the second piece during this period, you might wish to have your youth experience it prior to the Rite of Enrollment. Do whatever best suits the pastoral needs of your situation, as well as the schedules of all involved.

If you have not done this earlier in the *I Have Chosen You* process, obtain an index card from each candidate indicating the information regarding his/her sponsor. (Some pastors require that a sponsor procure a certificate from his/her pastor if not a member of the candidate's parish.) This will make your communication with sponsors much easier.

My Name _____

My Sponsor_____

Sponsor Address_____

      Parish_____

      Telephone _____

The group sessions during this "Period of Purification and Enlightenment" will focus on the four effects of confirmation enumerated in the Catechism, #1303:

Session 19—"...It deepens baptismal grace and unites us more firmly to Christ...

Session 20—"...(It)renders our bond with the Church more perfect...."

Session 21—"...(It) roots us more deeply in the divine filiation..."

Session 22—and gives us "special strength to spread and defend the faith by word and action."

Celebration of the Rite of Enrollment

This liturgy is celebrated, if possible, on a Sunday during Lent. We call this the liturgy of enrollment or election. We have already celebrated a "Rite of Choice" where the young people publicly symbolized their commitment to be a part of a confirmation preparation process. Today's liturgy (which should be a regular parish Sunday Mass) symbolizes the community's choosing, approving, and electing these young people into its full membership as adult, initiated Christians. Their catechist, sponsor, and parents should be present to also demonstrate their personal support and that of the faith community.

PROCESSION

Candidates and sponsors should be a part of the entrance procession and sit in a prominent place together in the church.

After the liturgy of the word (that concludes with the homily):

The leader (or D.R.E.) stands before the pastor and says:

> Father, I present to you these baptized young Christians who seek to deepen their Christian commitment and become full members of their church by receiving the sacrament of confirmation. They have been faithfully attending preparation sessions over these past __ months, have engaged in a service project to the community, and participated in a weekend retreat. As they enter into the final phase of their preparation I (we) ask that our parish community affirm and welcome them.

(Sponsors stand)

Pastor:

"Dear sponsors of these young people: Are you willing to undertake the task of guiding these candidates in the final phase of their preparation for confirmation?"

Sponsors:

"We are."

Pastor:

"Do you promise to support them by your prayers and example not only during these next weeks but throughout their lifetime?"

Sponsors:

"We do."

Pastor:

(To group leader[s] or D.R.E.): "Have you as their catechist(s) witnessed a desire in these young people to be more fully immersed in our parish community and that they have a real sense of commitment to following Jesus' way of life within the Roman Catholic Church?"

Leader(s) or D.R.E., (standing):

"I (We) have."

(Candidates stand)

Pastor:

"Young people of our parish: Do you desire to continue the process of Christian initiation begun in you at baptism, and continued in the Eucharist?"

Candidates:

"We do."

Pastor:

"Do you understand that the sacrament of confirmation symbolizes not a completion of your religious education but rather a deeper level of participation in the life of Christ and his church?"

Candidates:

"We do."

Pastor:

"Then may God bring to completion in you the good work that has begun in Jesus Christ. I invite you to come forward and to enroll your name in our parish book of candidates. (He then calls the name of each youth individually, who in turn enters the sanctuary with his or her sponsor, and enrolls his or her name in the book on a table next to the altar. The page is headed: "I promise to faithfully complete the Confirmation process I have begun in order to be fully initiated into the Catholic faith."

(When the last candidate has been enrolled, the pastor invites the congregation to applaud.)

Prayers for the Candidates

(Included in the Prayer of the Faithful)

Pastor:

"Let us pray for these young people as they enter the final phase of their preparation for confirmation."

Lector:

"For these young people that they feel in a concrete way the support of our parish community, let us pray to the Lord."

Congregation:

"Lord, hear our prayer."

Lector:

"That these young people may have the awareness that they have been especially chosen by God to receive the grace of this sacrament, let us pray to the Lord."

Congregation:

"Lord, hear our prayer."

Lector:

"For the parents, sponsors, catechists and all who have and continue to contribute to the spiritual formation of these candidates, let us pray to the Lord."

Congregation:

"Lord, hear our prayer."

Lector:

"For each of us, as we are mindful today of the gift of the Holy Spirit present in each of us, let us pray to the Lord."

Congregation:

"Lord, hear our prayer."

Pastor:

"Lord Jesus, we thank you for the witness here today of these beautiful young people who choose to follow you more closely. Give them your Spirit to guide, nourish, and sustain them all the days of their lives."

(The Mass then continues with the Creed.)

SPONSOR PAGE [this page may be copied and given to the sponsors]

Confirmation Sponsors

Who Can Be a Confirmation Sponsor?

First of all you should be a person of faith, a Roman Catholic adult who is an active member of the church. Ideally you are a member of the same parish as the young person you have been asked to sponsor (although this is not essential). And also you are someone who is willing to make a time commitment to this confirmation process called *I Have Chosen You.* But all this is probably the easy part.

The point is that it makes us very uncomfortable to be asked to guide another human being in the area of spirituality. We say: "Who am I? I'm not perfect! What right do I have?" And sometimes we go further with a kind of outdated or inaccurate understanding of humility. We say that it would be prideful for us to try to tell someone else, even a young person, how he or she should live a Christian life. But let's look more carefully and more honestly at why it is that we shrink from taking on this role. It is often for two reasons: one a good reason and the other a bad reason. The good reason is that we feel that we are no better or no holier than anyone else. This is true, and it's proper to feel this way. Nobody knows any more about God than anyone else. This fact should encourage us as sponsors, not discourage us! The bad reason is because we feel incompetent in the areas of theology and spirituality. We are "just lay people," not priests! "What do I know? I don't have a degree in theology or religious education." This feeling of intellectual inadequacy is a poor reason because theologians are not what young people need. What they need are friends for life's journey, friends who are just a few steps beyond on the road of experience and wisdom and the struggle to live in God's sight. And that's us—Christian adults. You may not believe this quite that easily, so we want to share with you some research on the topic of adults who minister well with youth.

The first study is an extensive survey developed by Search Institute in Minneapolis for seminary candidates throughout the country. The compilers of this research inquired of Christians of all ages what it was that they were looking for in the people who minister to them (in this case, the clergy). The responses basically boil down to two major ingredients: (1) an open, affirming, warm attitude toward people, and (2) an attitude toward a life filled with faith.

After these two primary considerations, the desirability of skills follows: ability to teach, counsel, organize, administer, and so forth. But notice that the major considerations have nothing to do with professional skills or academic background. Think about it a minute. What kind of person do you like to go to when you are going through a personal struggle? And who was it that you sought out for guidance in life or spirituality when you were a teenager? Or to put it another way: What type of adult individual did you look to and feel encouraged by in your own journey when you were a teenager?

The second piece of research is from the *Journal for the Scientific Study of Religion* (17:4, 1978). In an article by Hoge and Petrillo, "Determinants of Church Participation among High School Youth," two researchers surveyed 450 sophomores to try to figure out why they freely chose to participate in a church youth group. The first two reasons had to do with parents and peers. The third significant reason was that young people came to the group if the leader was (1) approachable, (2) sincere, and (3) expressed his or her own beliefs with self-assurance.

Notice again, an academic credential had nothing to do with it. Young people respond to someone who they feel likes them, is approachable, and is sincere—not a phony. So that's why it is a cop-out to say you can't work with them because you're not "qualified," if you equate qualifications with a certain educational background. If you mean that you don't like teenagers, and that you're not open, warm, sincere and affirming, and a person of faith—then you may have a point.

So the first step in becoming a sponsor for a young person is to believe that you can be helpful to a younger person just in virtue of your personality, plus the accumulation of life experience. Remember, they chose you, so they must already see these good qualities in you. It has nothing to do with being superior in any way to another person. It has to do with, to borrow from the definition of a sponsor in the Rite of Christian Initiation of Adults, a "friend for the journey."

Henri Nouwen, a preacher and writer in the areas of prayer and ministry, defines a minister as: "One who attempts to put one's own search for God, with all the moments of pain and joy, despair and hope, at the disposal of those who want to join this search but do not know how" (*Creative Ministry*, New York: Doubleday, 1971, p. 116). Teenagers are often people "who do not know how." And for us adults to put our own inner journeys with all their pain and joy "out on the table" for others to see requires a good deal of openness.

Let's add vulnerability to the list of qualifications needed for a spiritual ministry with youth. Often adults get uptight about sharing their struggles with adolescents because they feel it will weaken their image as a role model. Certainly at times there is a value in not revealing to a teenager some personal struggle we are experiencing. But most of the time, youth need to see that adults whom they like and respect are also people who have no easy time in living their lives. They need to hear that it's okay for them to struggle by hearing about your struggle. Rather than weaken an adult's image as a role model, it usually enhances it to share the truth because that inevitably wins the respect of anyone of any age. Henri Nouwen says that a minister needs to be a "wounded healer." By this he means that the best way to help another person find healing is for us to share in his or her "woundedness" by sharing our own. Lastly, let it be said that you have as much to gain during this process as does your candidate. It is a beautiful and rare opportunity to share your faith with another. It is bound to be a helpful and challenging experience for you also.

What Are You Being Asked to Do?

1. To attend the rite of enrollment at a Sunday liturgy.

2. To attend a special retreat program, "Journey in the Spirit," with candidates.

3. To attend the penance service, the rehearsal, and prayer service prior to confirmation and, of course, the celebration of confirmation itself.

4. To pray for the young person you are being asked to sponsor.

What Do You Do at the Liturgical Celebrations?

Just follow the simple directions to sponsors. You will receive copies of the "Rite of Enrollment" from your parish confirmation director.

SESSION 18: "Journey in the Spirit"

SPONSOR/CANDIDATE "MINI" RETREAT

Time: 2 hours

Materials needed:

Name tags and magic markers for each participant

Three index cards and a pen or pencil for each participant

Opening (20 minutes)

As people enter the room, have greeters at the door who welcome them and instruct them to put on a name tag.

Assign sponsors and candidates to sit as a pair in a group, or at a table with three other pairs (eight per group). Have a leader present at each table or group as a ninth member (who is neither a sponsor nor a candidate) to facilitate what occurs within the group. The leader should also welcome people as they arrive and introduce them to each other.

LARGE GROUP LEADER

The leader announces that this is a sponsor-candidate retreat, an opportunity for all to grow in faith while journeying today (or tonight) together.

ICEBREAKER

(10 minutes)

Using one ***index card,*** take a minute to jot down your most vivid memory of being in a church before the age of ten (or some other early childhood experience of religion). The leader invites participants to share contents of the card with the group.

SHARING

(10 minutes)

Write down two words on the ***second index card*** to describe God: the first word is how you thought of God as a child; the second word is how you think of God now in your life.

These words are shared within the individual groups.

WITNESS TALK: "JOURNEY IN THE SPIRIT"

(15 minutes)

This presentation could be delivered by any confirmed person. Perhaps a young adult who was confirmed a few years previous would be a good choice. The age of the speaker is not as important as the quality of the presentation. What is needed here is not a homily or lecture about confirmation. A desirable speaker is one who is willing to share personal life stories that reflect the struggle to grow, both humanly and spiritually, as he or she became fully initiated into the faith—the journey in the Spirit we all walk.

REFLECTION
(5 minutes)

On the **third index card** the participants write down a time in life when they felt God intervened, or, conversely, they could also write about the opposite of a religious experience if they feel they have not had one (i.e., a time when they needed God but felt that God remained at a distance). This should be done in silence in the group. To play recorded classical music in the background would be helpful in creating the desired atmosphere in the room.

DYADS
(10 minutes)

Break up the groups, pairing candidates with their own sponsors. Ask each pair, or dyad, to share with each other their reflection of God's intervention (or failure to intervene).

REFRESHMENT BREAK
(10 minutes)

SHORT TALK
(15 minutes)

At this time the D.R.E., pastor, youth minister, or confirmation program coordinator should address the group about the mentoring nature of the sponsor-candidate relationship, and how we all need someone to turn to on our faith journey. The people of the Christian community are this mutual support. The church today is calling upon sponsors to assist in the sacramental preparation of these young people.

PRAYER SERVICE
(15 minutes)

Begin with this guided meditation. Bring the entire group into a church—or else create an atmosphere in the meeting space by dimming the lights, lighting some candles, and perhaps drawing all of the chairs into a wide circle. Ask participants to close their eyes as the following meditation is read:

Imagine your spirit leaving your body and floating above you, through the roof to the outside, above this retreat house (place). It can be any time of day: the mellow expanse of sunlight at dawn or the sad shades of orange at sunset. The sky can be bright and blue, or gray and stormy, or it can be dark and crisp and peppered with a thousand stars. Choose whichever sky you want, whichever suits your mood, and allow your spirit to go soaring through it.

(Pause here for one full minute)

Travel now in your imagination through your sky, away and away until you come to the favorite place of your childhood, whatever that might be. It could be a tree, or a backyard, or a cottage, or your grandmother's kitchen. Remember what your favorite place was—and maybe still is—and be there now, all by yourself.

(Pause here for one full minute)

Allow Jesus to appear also at your favorite place. He stands before you, takes your hands and looks lovingly into your eyes. In your imagination visit with Jesus now.

(Pause here for one full minute)

Jesus calls you by name (pause briefly) and thanks you for being here today in order to grow in love and in maturity. He asks you how the days are going for you. He asks you about the risks you have taken or not taken today to step out in faith.

(Pause briefly)

He asks you if there is anything you need from him today to help you in your everyday life. Talk to Jesus now about what you need from him.

(Pause here for one full minute)

Jesus again holds your hands, looks into your eyes, and promises that he has heard your need and that he will respond and will help you. You are alone again in your favorite place but you feel differently because of your visit with Jesus. Let your spirit swiftly soar again in your sky, a sky which is the same, or perhaps a sky that has changed. Soar in that sky as far back as the distance you came, and allow your spirit to reenter those walls and reunite with your body (pause). Now open your eyes slowly.

SCRIPTURE READING
Choose one scripture from the following choices to be read aloud:

READINGS FROM THE OLD TESTAMENT
1. Isaiah 11:1–4a

   On him the Spirit of the Lord rests.

2. Isaiah 42:1–3

   I have endowed my servant with my Spirit.

3. Isaiah 61:1–3a, 6a, 8b, 9

   The Lord God has anointed me and has sent me to bring good news to the poor, to give them the oil of gladness.

4. Ezekiel 6:24–28

I will place a new Spirit in your midst.

5. Joel 2:23a, 26–30a (Hebrews 2:23a; 3:1–3a)

I will pour out my Spirit on all mankind.

READINGS FROM THE NEW TESTAMENT

1. Acts 1:3–8

You will receive the power of the Holy Spirit, and you will be my witnesses.

2. Acts 2:1–6, 14, 22b, 23, 32–33

They were all filled with the Holy Spirit, and began to speak in other languages.

3. Acts 8:1–4, 14–17

They laid hands on them, and they received the Holy Spirit.

4. Acts 10:1, 33–34a, 37–44

The Holy Spirit came down on all those listening to the word of God.

5. Acts 91:1b–6a

Did you receive the Holy Spirit when you became believers?

6. Romans 5:1–2, 5–8

The love of God has been poured into our hearts by the Holy Spirit which has been given to us.

7. Romans 8:14–7

The Spirit and our spirit bear united witness that we are children of God.

8. Romans 8:26–27

The Spirit himself will express our plea in a way that could never be put into words.

9. Corinthians 12:4–13

There is one and the same Spirit giving to each one as he chooses.

10. Galatians 5:16–17, 22–23a, 24–25

If we live in the Spirit, let us be directed by the Spirit.

11. Ephesians 1:3a, 4a, 13–19a

You have been signed with the seal of the Holy Spirit of the promise.

12. Ephesians 4:1–6

There is one body, one Spirit, and one baptism.

Closing Prayer: (Recite Together)

Spirit of God,
enlighten me
Grace of God
move me,
Heart of God,
electrify me
Compassion of God,
touch me
Hand of God,
heal me
Passion of God,
stir me
Mind of God,
counsel me.

SESSION 19: Faith

"Faith is a supernatural gift from God. In order to believe, man needs the interior help of the Holy Spirit" (CCC #179).

One definition of a catechist is as an "awakener of faith" in young—persons—first of faith in themselves, and also of faith in God. We have already discussed faith in the self. It is closely connected to the experience of faith in God. As mentioned earlier, James Fowler has done extensive research on the stages of faith. He feels that most adolescents are between what he calls the "synthetic conventional," where the young person's concerns are with the interpersonal, and the "individuative-reflective" stage, that begins at about age eighteen to twenty. In this latter stage the young adult views faith more and more as one's own and holds himself or herself responsible for commitments, lifestyles, beliefs, and attitudes.

The entire *I Have Chosen You* process is geared toward providing the needed reflection and community to nourish the young person toward this stage, or at least its beginnings. Prior to this maturation a teenager will probably have the experience of relying too much on a significant human being (or group) and buying into his or her values. The eventual disagreements with those whose values have been adopted help the young person to be more self-critical at how he or she has arrived at these beliefs. This disillusionment is inevitable, although painful, if the young person is to grow. It will probably impact faith in God, in that a young person may have difficulty in trusting in general during this time. For Fowler, faith is not a noun but a verb because it involves relating to "someone" in a way that invests our heart, our care, and our hope. Faith is a trusting commitment.

In the Introductory pages, we discussed that John Westerhoff distinguishes between "religion" (faith's expression) and "faith" that is deeply personal, dynamic, and ultimate. Educationally, religion is a means and faith is the end. Faith cannot be taught by any method of instruction. For Westerhoff, faith is "taught" by the experience of a faith-filled community. This means sharing experience, story telling, celebration, action, and reflection in the context of community—all ingredients of the *I Have Chosen You* process. For adolescents he feels that what he calls "affiliative" faith is crucial. This is the feeling that we belong to a real community and that through our active participation we can make a contribution to its life.

And so we invite young people to see the value in themselves. We also help them to have a genuine experience of being a part of the faith community. We present faith as a gift and as the grace to believe in the reality of God. We also present faith as a challenge to care about the things to which Jesus calls us. It also involves a commitment to trust, like Abraham, that God will care for us throughout our lives and eventually bring us to heaven, our "promised" land. Last, let's look at the "images" we have of God and Jesus which impact our faith life and which we will be asking our group to examine during this session.

When we were little children we may have read books that showed pictures of God as a grandfather with a flowing white beard. Artists drew these pictures to give children the idea that God was kind and loving. When it came to portraying Jesus, these artists tried to emphasize his great gentleness. That would have been a fine approach, except that, unwittingly, they made a big mistake. Our culture had mistakenly categorized gentleness as primarily a feminine characteristic. So how was Jesus portrayed in these paintings and statues? Oftentimes it was as a physically delicate man. Nothing could be further from the truth.

Jesus grew up in a small town, lived a simple life, and worked with his hands. He kept himself in good condition. When he was thirty he was able to hike up and down his country over rough, rocky terrain, sleeping outdoors, spending long days responding to crowds, and frequently giving several hours to prayer late at night. He could not have done these things unless he had had physical strength. We must reject these weak images of our Savior because they are not true and can be harmful to us. Jesus' gentleness was a strength, not a weakness.

Sometimes parents, in their efforts to teach obedience to their children, will reinforce an inappropriate idea of God. They will speak about him as someone who sees everything the children do—especially the bad things. In this instance the frightened little children probably do what they are told, but long after the incident they carry around with them this image of God as a severe judge or policeman, ready to pounce on them the minute they make a mistake. Even certain Bible stories, taken out of context, can give wrong ideas of God. Children who hear these stories without proper explanation can imagine God as being mean and vindictive and causing disasters.

The first ideas that children have about most things are partial, incomplete, and somewhat inaccurate. As children grow their ideas are filled out and corrected. But sometimes this development doesn't take place, and then there is trouble—especially if the mistaken notions deal with God and Jesus, or their relationship to us. A person can be a maturing teenager and still think of God as an old man or a fragile person or an avenging judge. These are not very appealing images. If that is what we think of God or Jesus, no wonder we have no desire to develop a relationship in faith.

Session 14 discussed how important it is to have a true image of oneself. If our relationship with God is to be worth anything it is equally important to have a true image of him. As we look into this we realize that some people have another difficulty in thinking about God—it's the question of where God is.

Talking about God in terms of spatial images poses many problems. Up until modern times people had thought of the sky as a mysterious region. Even with our space probes and our knowledge of astronomy, some of the aura of mystery still clings to the notion of the sky or the heavens—especially when we bring in religious ideas. Many people, when thinking of Jesus' conception and birth, figure that somehow he came down out of the sky and then was born of Mary at Bethlehem. Then the story of the ascension at the end of his life can give the impression that at that time he was lifted back up into the sky from which he had come. The problem with this type of thinking is that the sky is a long way off. If God and Jesus are imagined so far away, an important truth can slip away from us. We continue to believe that God is everywhere—including here in our midst—but we begin to feel that he is a long distance away from us. This leads to other feelings associated with distance. We feel that God is indifferent to us, or doesn't understand us, or is too occupied with more important matters to care about us.

Like hope and love, faith is a "theological" virtue; these three are the essence of the spiritual life according to St. Paul (1 Thessalonians 1:3; 5:8; 1 Corinthians 13:13). Faith is a gift of God to the individual. The church distinguishes it from but connects it to "morals" or behavior. Revealed truths are believed in faith and move us to the way God wants us to live. The church also distinguishes between faith and reason. These are not at odds, but faith means that we believe without perceptible proof. The church also connects faith with good works or action. Faith without works is dead (James 2:26). Faith means "coming to know God's love, greatness, and majesty...living in thanksgiving...knowing the unity and true dignity of all men...making good use of created things...and trusting in God in every circumstance" (CCC excerpts #223–227).

JOURNAL EXERCISE

Do Exercise # 1, "Who Is Your God?"/ "Where Is Your God?" and Exercise # 2, "How Deep Is Your Faith?" in the Journal, Session 19.

DISCUSSION QUESTIONS

1. Did you ever feel you were asked to take a risk in faith?

2. Do you feel that God will take care of you if you just try to do the right thing?

Note: At the end of this session are some prayers that candidates for confirmation should memorize, if they have not already done so. You might wish to recite them together as your closing prayer for this session.

SESSION 20: The Church

"The Church is in history, but at the same time she transcends it. It is only 'with the eyes of faith' that one can see her in her visible reality and at the same time in her spiritual reality as the bearer of divine life" (CCC #770).

> **They devoted themselves to the apostles' teaching and fellowship, to the breaking of bread and the prayers. Awe came upon everyone, because many wonders and signs were being done by the apostles. All who believed were together and had all things in common; they would sell their possessions and goods and distribute the proceeds to all, as any had need. Day by day, as they spent much time together in the temple, they broke bread at home and ate their food with glad and generous hearts, praising God and having the goodwill of all the people. And day by day the Lord added to their number those who were being saved. (Acts 2:42–47)**

In many sessions of **I Have Chosen You** we have discussed various aspects of the Catholic Church. In this session we will focus on a few models of church, the institutional church, and religious and priestly vocations within the church. Begin this session by brainstorming the word *church*. Have each person say the first word that comes to mind. After this is over go back and ask why the word was chosen. For many people "church" conjures up an image of a place or an institution with laws and government. In his book, *Models of the Church*, Avery Dulles, S.J. (New York: Image Books, 1991) suggests five major images which describe the church: community, herald, institution, sacrament, and servant. Each image sheds some light on the mystery of the church (see Journal page in Session 20 for more detail). In preparation for this session we recommend a perusal of the Catechism, Chapter Three, Article 9. It discusses the church's origin, foundation, and mission. The church is described as the "people of God," the "body of Christ," and the "Temple of the Holy Spirit." The four characteristics or "marks" of the church are that it is "one," "holy," "catholic" (meaning universal), and "apostolic."

It is impossible in the short space of this session to cover the span of church history. We have provided a simple outline, however, which reviews the most significant events of our Roman Catholic heritage (also in the Journal). St. Ignatius, an early bishop and martyr, first called the Christian Church "Catholic." The first eight hundred years of the church are dominated by the "Fathers of the Church"—its early thinkers, writers, and leaders. They were very crucial in correcting errors (called heresies) which crept into the church. It was a period that clarified the self-understanding of the church. Church "councils" were called to correct heresies and set directions for the Catholic community. The pope can call an ecumenical ("worldwide") council whenever he feels it is necessary. Also, in the early centuries of church life we have the development of monasticism. This began with unmarried men and women going to the desert to live as hermits totally devoted to prayer. Gradually they began to join together and live in communities called monasteries. St. Benedict was an early monastic leader who wrote a famous and still practiced "rule" for a community to follow (A.D. 520).

Today in the church we have many vocations. We have clergy or "priests" who are trained in theology and ministry to lead our communities, called parishes. The priest who leads the parish is called the pastor. Included in the clergy, or clerical state of life, are deacons—men who are ordained to assist in some priestly duties. Deacons may be married, but church practice has required celibacy (the unmarried state) of its priests for many centuries in order that they might devote themselves totally to ministry. From the clergy are chosen bishops who have the authority to supervise and govern geographical collections of parishes, called dioceses. (Ask the candidates if they know the name of their bishop and diocese.) From the bishops are chosen cardinals to assist at the highest level of church authority at the Vatican, the center of church government in Rome. The pope is elected, usually from the college (group) of cardinals, as the supreme head of the church, the successor of St. Peter the Apostle.

Laity or lay people form the bulk of the church's population. Many are married, many are single, some are children and teenagers. Some dedicate their lives or a part of their life to full-time service as lay missioners or lay volunteers. Still others dedicate their entire lives to service by joining religious communities as Religious Brothers or Religious Sisters. These people take vows to be celibate, not to own private property, or have private income (the vow of poverty), and to be obedient to their superiors. Many of these Brothers and Sisters are teachers, nurses, social workers, catechists, and missionaries (a priest can also be a member of a religious community). Finally, some lay people choose a contemplative, monastic lifestyle devoted to silence and prayer. These people also take vows and are called monks and nuns. Young people should be encouraged to consider seriously a vocation as a member of the church.

The Catholic Church is the family of God on earth into which a person is born by baptism. Its purpose is to build up the kingdom of God on earth in a community of love. It is also called the "mystical body of Christ." A beautiful and significant description of the church can be found in the *Dogmatic Constitution on the Church* from the documents of Vatican Council II.

JOURNAL EXERCISE

Review charts "Models of the Church" and "Synopsis of Highlights of Church History" with your group, in the Journal, Session 20. If you need some help in understanding these better, ask your parish priest or director of religious education.

A suggestion for this session:

Invite into your group a person in full-time ministry in the church: a priest, sister, brother, deacon, or lay volunteer. (If no full-time minister is available, invite someone who has a part-time ministry, such as a eucharistic minister or member of the parish pastoral council.) Allow half of the time for this session for guests to speak about their lifestyle and what the church means to them.

DISCUSSION QUESTIONS

1. Which priest or religious (or other minister within the Church) has had an impact on you?

2. Would you consider giving a year or two of your life to voluntary service within the church, either in this country or in a foreign land? Do you ever think about having a calling to the priesthood or religious life yourself?

SESSION 21: Trust in God

"Jesus asks for childlike abandonment to the providence of our heavenly Father who takes care of his children's smallest needs..." (CCC #305).

> **Immediately he made the disciples get into the boat and go on ahead to the other side, while he dismissed the crowds. And after he had dismissed the crowds, he went up to the mountain by himself to pray. When evening came, he was there alone, but by this time the boat, battered by the waves, was far from the land, for the wind was against them. And early in the morning he came walking toward them on the sea. But when the disciples saw him walking on the sea, they were terrified, saying, "It is a ghost!" And they cried out in fear. But immediately Jesus spoke to them and said "Take heart, it is I; do not be afraid." Peter answered him, "Lord, if it is you, command me to come to you on the water." He said, "Come." So Peter got out of the boat, started walking on the water, and came toward Jesus. But when he noticed the strong wind, he became frightened, and beginning to sink, he cried out, "Lord, save me!" Jesus immediately reached out his hand and caught him, saying to him, "You of little faith, why did you doubt?" When they got into the boat, the wind ceased. And those in the boat worshiped him, saying, "Truly you are the Son of God." (Matthew 14:22–33)**

Let's start by saying that God does not usually contradict the forces of nature he has established. Therefore, this miracle must be considered a very special one, meant to teach a universal lesson. The lesson, of course, is that of trust. Peter's problem was that he did not dare put his entire confidence in Jesus' invitation to come to him.

One question this raises for us is: How willing are we to put our trust in other people? Do we really believe that people care about us, that they enjoy being with us, that they love us? Or do we doubt other people by always asking ourselves questions about their sincerity and motivation?

If we distrust others, it is usually because we have had some bad experience along life's way. Perhaps we once told a secret to someone and the person betrayed us. Maybe we once thought someone was our friend and that person hurt us. Maybe a parent or some other significant adult in our lives really let us down. After bad experiences like these, the human temptation is to crawl into a shell. But this leads to loneliness and isolation, and increases our misery.

For young people it is necessary to learn that human beings are fallible, and to learn this requires disappointment. The parents they once idealized are discovered to have "feet of clay." The friends they cherish are weak and capable of failing them. Even the persons with whom they are romantically involved will eventually be discovered to be human! These discoveries, although painful, are a necessary part of growth and will teach young people a great deal about trust, as well as the perennial fidelity of the Lord.

Often teenagers suffer because of worry about situations over which they're helpless. They have not come to appreciate the comforting words in the gospel that it does not add a single cubit to a person's stature to worry over anything, and that the worries of today are sufficient because there's nothing that we can do about tomorrow anyway. Kevin, age seventeen, wrote: "When I think of suffering, I think of mental suffering rather than a physical one. It seems that the suffering that I have remembered in my life was more mental suffering. When my parents divorced I think I suffered. Two people I loved very much didn't seem to love each other. The pain and suffering I felt inside seemed much worse than any physical suffering I can ever remember experiencing." A year or so after the divorce of his parents Kevin reported that he was counseling a friend who was undergoing a similar sort of suffering. Kevin at that time remarked to his peer that there are certain situations in life over which we have no control and that what we have to learn to do is accept them rather than worry why they are the way that they are. Kevin advanced a giant step during that year and the wisdom of his counsel to this friend could be of solace to many a teenager. Young people simply find life's situations difficult to accept and churn within themselves the question, "Why is this so?"

Main sources of worry to the teenager are the school, the family, economic survival, and the precariousness of life in our sometimes violent world. Another major source of worry is how one looks physically to the opposite sex and how one is maturing physically in relationship to peers. Sexuality too is a source of worry, and for many teenagers this topic is difficult to discuss with parents. Also, adolescents need to be successful in some way, and feelings of inadequacy, real or imagined, can be sources of much anxiety.

Trust in life and in human beings usually parallels our trust in God. Trust, psychologists tell us, is the most crucial stage of our infancy, and the security which will sustain us for a lifetime is established in our early childhood. Some teenagers have had painful experiences with parents (or other significant adults) when they were very young and may not have yet completed the developmental task of establishing trust in people. Hopefully their sharing groups in this confirmation preparation will help these individuals to establish a deeper inner security. Also, the retreat experiences as well as the sponsor relationship can help greatly in this area.

But despite any insecurities we have, despite any scars from childhood, each of us can learn and nourish an inner reliance upon the Lord. The word *faith* in the Old Testament does not only mean an intellectual belief in God's existence, but also a trust in his continual help and guidance. The more we talk with Jesus in prayer, the more risks we take by giving the problems to him which we carry in our hearts, the more we will grow in trust. (Conclude the prayer time with a reading of Psalm 139.)

JOURNAL EXERCISE
Do Exercises #1 and #2, "How Much Trust Do You Have?" in the Journal, Session 21.

DISCUSSION QUESTIONS
1. What is it that increases your trust in people?

2. What increases your trust in God?

SESSION 22
PART A
The Holy Spirit

"By his Death and Resurrection, Jesus is constituted in glory as Lord and Christ. From his fullness, he poured out the Holy Spirit on the apostles and the Church. The Holy Spirit, whom Christ the head pours out on his members, builds, animates, and sanctifies the Church..." (CCC 746–47).

(Special Note: A complete Bible is needed for this session.)

The mystery of God is not something we can intellectually grasp like an article of philosophy. No, God is the one for "in him we live and move and have our being" (Acts 17:28). And so the Spirit is the ground of our being. There is a word in Hebrew, *ruah*, which means "wind," "breath," "spirit," or "power." We also read in Genesis (2:7) that it is *ruah* which gives us life as human beings. In the Jewish Scriptures the prophets, such as Joel, Ezekiel, and Isaiah, talk about the "spirit":

> **The spirit of the Lord God is upon me,**
> **because the Lord has anointed me;**
> **he has sent me to bring good news to the oppressed,**
> **to bind up the brokenhearted,**
> **to proclaim liberty to the captives,**
> **and release to the prisoners... (Isaiah 61:1)**

(Jesus himself repeats these words of Isaiah in the synagogue at Nazareth [Luke 4:18].)

In the New Testament we read that the conception of Jesus in Mary's womb is brought about by the overshadowing of the Holy Spirit (Luke 1:35). When Jesus begins his public ministry we read that he is baptized by John in the Jordan River and John saw **"the Spirit of God descending like a dove [and] coming upon him"** (Matthew 3:16). Jesus talks about the Spirit when the Pharisee Nicodemus comes to learn from Jesus at night: **"Amen, amen I say to you, no one can enter the kingdom of God without being born of water and Spirit"** (John 3:5).

Finally, at the Last Supper Jesus tells his followers that he is leaving them but that the Father is sending another helper to be with them, "the Spirit of truth" (John 14:17). We find this prophecy of Jesus fulfilled on Pentecost Sunday when the apostles heard a loud noise and something appeared to them that seemed like tongues of fire: "And they were all filled with the holy Spirit" (Acts 2:4). It is at Pentecost that Peter addresses the crowd and quotes from a prophecy of Joel: "It will come to pass in the last days, God says, that I will pour out a portion of my spirit upon all flesh" (Acts 2:17). Peter is saying that that time had arrived (and is still here now). The epistles also, the letters of the apostles (especially St. Paul), are filled with references to the Spirit, as we shall see in the exercise on the "fruits" of the Holy Spirit.

We can see from these scriptural references how various symbolic images have affected Christian art. We often see the Spirit portrayed as a dove or a flame. This ought not to limit our religious imagination nor our understanding of the meaning of God's Spirit in our lives. The "Spirit" of God is not some abstract philosophical concept which we can grasp; it is a mystery in which we live. Also, the Holy Spirit is received at our baptism, but we are plunged into the fullness of the gift of the Spirit at our confirmation.

The Holy Spirit (sometimes called the "Holy Ghost") is the third person of the Blessed Trinity. He is the "sanctifier" because he makes us holy by the graces and virtues he gives us. He is also called the "comforter" because he continually comforts and nourishes the church.

JOURNAL EXERCISE

Do Exercise#1, "The Holy Spirit" and Exercise #2, "Fruits of the Spirit" in the Journal, Session 22.

DISCUSSION QUESTION

1. What has been your image or understanding of the Holy Spirit since you were a young child?

PART B
Challenge to Witness

Traditionally we have associated confirmation with a strengthening in the Holy Spirit and sometimes in the past we used militaristic terms such as "soldier of Christ" to denote this. To focus on the Holy Spirit as a prophetic, strengthening force, we are going to look at some of the Old Testament prophets. These were people who arose during the latter period of Israel's history after the kingdom had crumbled. Today we use the word *prophet* to mean someone who forecasts the future. In the Bible a prophet is someone who looks at the present and critiques and challenges others to keep God's (Yahweh's) law. The prophets are ordinary people who feel a special calling to speak out as God's spokespersons. After the kingdom divided in 932 B.C. following Solomon's death, we find prophets in both the north and south. In the north, three famous prophets are Amos, Jonah, and Hosea. Amos, a herdsman, criticizes the way wealthy people neglect and abuse poor people. Many of his messages ring very true in affluent Christian nations today. Jonah is the "reluctant" prophet. Sent on a mission by God, Jonah gets on a boat going in the opposite direction. Even though scripture scholars believe this story to be fictional, it is full of meaning and teaches important lessons. Hosea is the third prophet of the north we are considering. In his own life Hosea had the experience of an unfaithful wife named Gomer. This infidelity forms the basis of his discussion of Israel and the unfaithful spouse of Yahweh who keeps breaking the covenant.

In the south we have the prophet Jeremiah, also a reluctant prophet, who tries to use his youth as an excuse for not speaking out for God. The book of Jeremiah is the longest book in the Bible. The prophet Ezekiel, who arises when the Israelites are in captivity in Babylon, has the famous "vision of the dry bones" where the Spirit restores life to the community. We have selected passages to read in your group to give the young people a feel for the prophetic mission. By looking at the prophets, the candidates for confirmation will get a sense of the kind of strengthening that the Spirit gives. It is a strengthening to speak out if need be, to challenge others when God's ways are being ignored. It's the same Spirit that was very clear in Jesus' mission in Jewish society. He had the inner strength to be true to his convictions even though it led to his eventual death.

Sometimes the Spirit does not so much move us to speak out as it does to silently be true to what we know we should do and be as a follower of Jesus Christ. As Paul writes to Timothy: "For the Spirit that God has given us does not make us timid; instead his Spirit fills us with power, love and self-control. Do not be ashamed, then, of witnessing for our Lord" (2 Timothy 1:6–8). Today, instead of saying "prophetic force" we speak of being a "witness" for Jesus Christ. This means that by the way we conduct our lives, by our actions, and by our words, we are demonstrating the values of the gospel. For adolescents struggling to be themselves in a world fraught with many dangers and evil influences, this strengthening in the Holy Spirit is a very timely and maturing religious experience.

"God continues to manifest himself through the Holy Spirit at work in the world, and especially in the Church. Christ, risen and living, is present to believers through the power of the Spirit....The Spirit's actions also makes believers sensitive to God's promptings in their hearts, moving them to respond and bear witness to him so that others, too, may come to know the Lord." (National Catechetical Directory, #54)

DISCUSSION QUESTION

1. Have you ever felt that either you yourself, or someone else whom you know (or know of), was "moved by the Spirit?" When and where did you observe this?

CLOSING PRAYER

Pass around the Bible and do the readings outlined in the Journal, Session 22, "The Holy Spirit: Challenge to Witness."

Note: If you did not have time to discuss confirmation names previously, do so at this session.

SESSION 23: "Christian Story" Retreat

(Time frame: a weekend: 7:00 P.M. Friday—12 noon Sunday/Suggested month: January or February, before Lent)

As we journey toward the final step of Christian initiation, this weekend retreat is constructed to help the candidates examine their own life experience and personal faith (their personal "Christian Story") and to reflect on it in the light of the Christian community's story and vision. How does their life experience relate to Christianity? What appreciation do they have of their faith, and what practical decisions have they made about living a life of faith? These are the goals of the weekend.

Important note: Each retreatant should bring a New Testament and the *I Have Chosen You* Journal. Radios, "walk-mans," cell phones, pagers, lap-top computers, and other electronic devices are not allowed. If a cell phone or pager is required in case of a family emergency, the retreatant should discuss the matter with an adult leader.

THE TEAM
The team of the retreat would ideally be a few teenagers already confirmed, some young adults who are a bit further along the road than the retreatants in their journey with Jesus, and also some older adults. As far as the small group meetings, they should be led by two team members, someone older and someone younger.

Friday

Arrival/name tags (if group is large enough to warrant them).

7:00 P.M.
Welcome by leader who explains the theme of the weekend and gives some practical information.

7:15 P.M.
"Name Game"

All of the exercises on the retreat will presume that we are dealing with the merger of at least two confirmation groups, or at least twenty youth retreatants. If the retreat is being conducted for one small group of eight to twelve, adapt the directions so that all exercises are done within that one small group of eight to twelve (or two small equal groups of five to six, plus team members). Have the group make an outer circle and an inner circle facing each other. The leader will announce to each pair an item to be discussed between them for 30 to 60 seconds. When the leader blows his whistle to signal that the time is ended, everyone on the outer circle takes one step to the right to face a new person while the inner circle remains stationary. The item to be discussed by each pair is: "Will you retain your baptismal name or will you choose another name at confirmation? If you choose another name, why? And what name do you think it will be?"

7:45 P.M.
"Dyads": Divide the retreatants in pairs (trying to pair the people who know each other least) and assign them to private rooms, or a private corner of a large room. Each pair should answer for each other: "Who is the per-

son in your life whom you feel has had the biggest impact on you in terms of impressing you with their faith in God?" When the bell is rung in 10 minutes all should return to the large group.

8:05 P.M.

Talk #1—"My Story" (speakers may choose to begin or close with an appropriate, reflective recorded song).

This talk is best given by a slightly older teenager. In it he or she traces his or her life experience by means of a life graph (see Exercise #1 sheet at end of retreat material). Starting with the first grade the speaker talks about his or her life, its ups and downs, its crises and challenges, its joys and hopes for the future. The speaker should tie in his or her own confirmation to the graph. This talk will set the tone of the entire retreat weekend.

8:30 P.M.

Large group—"Group Division"

The adult in charge should divide the group into small groups of six to eight participants and assign two team members to the group. The team should have decided at their planning sessions with whom they wish to work.

8:35 P.M.

Small groups: Complete and share your own individual life graphs as a means of sharing your own "story," Exercise #1 in retreat materials.

9:30 P.M.

Break

9:45 P.M.

Talk #2—By the adult leading the retreat.

This short talk should sum up the purpose of this retreat as building a community by sharing our stories and looking at Jesus' message that sheds light on our own lives. If we are all confirmation candidates we are saying that we wish to belong more fully to the church. The church, as we already studied, is a community of believers living together in Christian love. But the building of community is work, and that is why everyone's cooperation, openness, and sharing is needed this weekend. Hopefully this retreat will be a microcosm of what the church really is.

10:00 P.M.

Night Prayer

Have retreatants sit on the floor in a large circle in the conference room; light a candle in the center of the circle.

Open with a reflective recorded song.

> Reading: *One Solitary Life:*
> He was born in an obscure village,
> The child of a peasant woman.

He grew up in still another village,
Where he worked in a carpenter shop until he was thirty.
Then for three years he was an itinerant preacher.
He never wrote a book.
He never held an office.
He never had a family or owned a house.
He didn't go to college.
He never visited a big city.
He never traveled two hundred miles from the place where he was born.
He did none of the things one usually associates with greatness.
He had no credentials but himself.
He was only thirty-three when the tide of public opinion turned against him.
His friends ran away.
He was turned over to his enemies and went through the mockery of a trial.
He was nailed to a cross between two thieves.
While he was dying, his executioners gambled for his clothing,
The only property he had on earth.
When he was dead, he was laid in a borrowed grave through the pity of a friend.
Nineteen centuries have come and gone
And today he is the central figure of the human race and the leader of mankind's progress.
All the armies that ever marched,
All the navies that ever sailed,
All the parliaments that ever sat,
All the kings that ever reigned,
Put together,
Have not affected the life of man on this earth as much as that

ONE SOLITARY LIFE.

Leader: Talk about the fact that tonight we have all shared personally about our lives. Jesus, because he was human as well as divine, knows the feeling of every struggle we could possibly have. Invite all to share (aloud if possible, or if not aloud, then within their hearts) with God and with the group one area of their life where they are in need of God's help or healing. (Team members should set the tone by being prepared to share tonight aloud.)

After the sharing is completed have the circle join hands and ask everyone to pray the Lord's Prayer for all the needs that have been mentioned.

10:45 P.M.
Recreation time

11:30 P.M.
To sleeping area

12:00 MIDNIGHT

Lights out. (Sleep is essential for active participation throughout the weekend. The young people should not be allowed to stay up talking throughout the night. A curfew needs to be firmly established.)

SATURDAY

7:15 A.M.

Rising bell

7:45 A.M.

Morning prayer

Opening Song

A few moments of quiet meditation.

Reading: **Ephesians 3:14–19**

A few more moments of silence.

Closing Prayer:

> To the beginning of this day you have brought us, O Lord Almighty. Preserve us now by your power so that throughout this whole day we may not fall into any sin; rather, that all our words, thoughts, and acts may become part of your holy, providential plan. This we ask of you through our Lord Jesus Christ, your Son, who lives and reigns with you in the unity of the Holy Spirit, God forever. Amen
>> From *The Short Breviary*,
>> (Liturgical Press, 1962, p. 134)

8:00 A.M.

Breakfast

9:00 A.M.

Warm-up song. To loosen up the group we suggest you do one or two songs. You may wish to embellish the lyrics by adding some comical gestures. Suggestions: "Old Macdonald Had a Farm," "Rise and Shine,"—any song, new or old, which is well known and spirited will do.

9:20 A.M.

Talk #3—"The Masks I Wear" (best given by an older, confirmed teenager).

This talk deals with the struggle to be oneself. While acknowledging the need for some degree of defensiveness and protection from total vulnerability, the speaker points out the detrimental aspects of wearing false fronts or facades. The speaker shares some of his or her own "masks," and the accompanying reasons for the fears of being oneself. Peer pressure and expectations will account for some of this, as well as the stereotypes which are demanded by society. The speaker concludes the talk by explaining that the retreat experience is a microcosm of the Christian community. In this community it is "okay" to be oneself because it is a place of acceptance, trust, and love.

9:45 A.M.
Small group: Complete and share the mask exercise (see Exercise #2 sheet in retreat material).

10:45 A.M.
Break

11:15 A.M.
A Guided Meditation: An adult leads this exercise. (The exercise should be done on a carpeted floor, if possible, so that people may lie down; if this is not possible, then use a comfortable sitting position.)

Introduction by Leader: As we get older there are so many more ways to pray than we knew as a child. Being a teenager you are probably into some good music. An excellent way to start to pray is to play a song to get your mind off all the everyday realities. (Play a quiet classical song, or any soothing music without lyrics.) So try to start praying by letting go of all the pressures you have. (Ask retreatants to lie on the floor, bodies not touching, with eyes closed.)

Steps to Relaxation

(Read each step slowly, pausing between sentences.)

1. Relax yourself by breathing in and out, slowly. Do this seven or eight times.

2. Picture yourself standing at the edge of the sea in the late afternoon. The sun is setting in the horizon and the only sounds you hear are the waves crashing onto the shore and the distant call of seagulls. You are the only person standing on the beach which stretches as far as you can see.

3. In the distance, way out on the water, you see a shadowy figure of a person. It slowly moves closer toward you and you recognize the long hair and bearded face and long white robe. You realize that it is Jesus, your Lord, and he seems to be heading straight toward you.

4. However, he suddenly stops out on the water and he calls your name and looks into your eyes. He is several hundred feet offshore. He opens his arms and says to you, "Come to me." (Pause here for a few minutes of silence)

5. Slowly you stand and walk to the water's edge. You look again at his outstretched arms and inviting eyes. You start to walk into the chilly water. (Pause)

6. Suddenly you find yourself walking on the water, getting closer and closer to Jesus. He's saying something to you. What is he saying? (Pause) Now you are very close and look into his eyes. He takes both of your hands. How do you feel? Who is speaking? What is being said?

7. Discuss with Jesus that you are preparing to receive the sacrament of confirmation. How does he feel about that? What does he say to you about it?

8. After you have visited with Jesus for a few more moments, open your eyes very slowly and return in your mind to where you are. Now you may sit up (give time for this step #8 to gradually occur).

Conclude: This type of prayer is meditation guided by these eight images. It is one way of praying. There are all kinds of settings in which you can use your God-given imagination to have a conversation with Jesus. After reading a gospel story you might want to try to put yourself into the same scene in relation to Jesus. Or a place in nature (such as the shore) might be more helpful. The important thing is that your imagination is used to help you to talk more personally with your Lord.

11:45 A.M.
Prepare for lunch

12:00 P.M.
Lunch

12:30 P.M.
Recreation/free time

(This is a good time for the team to meet to assess the retreat thus far. Is there any youth who seems depressed or isolated, on the periphery of the group? Is there someone who is not participating? Is there any difficulty in any small group? Do any schedule changes seem in order? Close the meeting with a short group prayer for the retreatants.)

2:00 P.M.
Individual Meditations: The team ahead of time has written the chapter/verse of a particular gospel story, or lines from one of the epistles, and put it in a sealed envelope with the name of a retreatant on the envelope; these are distributed and silence in the house is requested until the bell rings at 2:40 when they are to report to their small group. They should take their New Testament, journals, and a pen and go to their room, to the chapel, outside, or to some private corner in the house and read their assigned passage in faith as having something to say to them personally about their own lives. This reflection should be jotted down briefly in their journals. They should talk to no one during this brief silent period of reflection. Adult leaders will need to walk around the retreat house and grounds to ensure that this silence is being maintained.

2:40 P.M.
Ring bell—assemble large group.

2:45 P.M.

Small groups: Share journals and/or the "fruit" of your individual meditations, Exercise #3 in retreat materials.

3:30 P.M.

Break

3:50 P.M.

Talk #4—"Friendship With Jesus Christ"

This talk is best given by a young adult.

This is a talk with a specifically "faith" focus. The speaker should begin by discussing the qualities of human friendship, giving examples from his or her own life. Then these same qualities should be translated to a relationship with Jesus that, like any other friendship, is a two-way street! (A favorite gospel story would be appropriate during this talk.) The speaker could point out difficulties that he or she is experiencing (or has experienced in the past) in relating to the Lord. In conclusion, retreatants should be challenged as candidates for confirmation to get closer to Jesus by reading his gospel daily (which is Jesus' story), and spending time in prayer regularly.

4:15 P.M.

Small groups: Share "Jesus Exercise" (see Exercise #4 sheet in retreat materials).

5:15 P.M.

Break

5:30 P.M.

Liturgy (if possible). The team should plan a meaningful liturgy with special songs and readings in conjunction with the celebrant. If a eucharistic liturgy is not possible, an alternative would be to return as a group for a parish liturgy in the late afternoon or early evening on Sunday.

6:30 P.M.

Supper/free time

7:30 P.M.

Short song fest or some other "icebreaker" activity decided on by the team

7:45 P.M.

Large group sharing: This is an opportunity for any retreatant or team member to say openly anything he or she wishes about the retreat weekend thus far: a feeling, an insight, an observation, a criticism, a source of confusion, an aspiration, a wish. A team member should open the sharing to set the tone.

8:35 P.M.

Talk #5—"Confirming Each Other" (by a teen, young adult, or adult).

A synonym for the verb "to confirm" (in a non-sacramental sense) is "to affirm." In a sense we are all "sacraments" for each other when we confirm or affirm each other as good and lovable persons. By doing so we build the Christian community. In this talk the speaker focuses on the deep need in all people to be affirmed as worthwhile. This need begins in infancy where it is extremely important to experience human warmth. The speaker should stress the importance of physical touch as a means of affirming each other and dismiss the taboos of our society which is so quick to attach a sexual connotation to every action. The self-sufficiency of the macho image for males can also be discussed as a not-too-human approach toward other people. The speaker should continue to point out other means of affirmation (e.g., a look, a smile, a remark, or compliment) and personally describe the ones that make a person feel better about himself or herself. The temptation to put ourselves down, and the challenge to graciously receive positive strokes and to believe in them are relevant to this topic. In conclusion the speaker could point out that Jesus' mission in the gospel was largely that of affirmation—and that he spent much of his time helping people to feel better about themselves. A good example would be the story of the woman caught in adultery (John 8:1–11).

9:00 P.M.

(Large group): confirmation posters

A poster paper is taped on the back of each retreatant. The group is instructed to go to everyone in the room and write one positive comment on the paper without signing it. Appropriate music about friendship, love, or community can be played in the background. When everyone is finished, the group should be instructed to sit on the floor and read their posters quietly in the spirit of receiving a gift. (Materials needed: large newsprint, magic markers for everybody, masking tape)

9:45 P.M.

Break

10:00 P.M.

Night prayer. The large group sits in a dimly-lit room again with a candle, crucifix, and New Testament in the center of the circle.

Opening Song: Play a religious song to set the mood for prayer.

Reading: A team member goes to center and reads, from the New Testament, **John 14:15–29**.

A few moments of silence; then another team member takes the crucifix from the center. Leader: We are now going to pass around a crucifix and we ask each of you to take it and look at it for a few short moments and pray in your own way, out loud or silently in your heart, whichever you prefer, and then pass the crucifix on to the person next to you.

(A few team members should be seated together to begin the passing of the cross in order to model how to pray aloud for the retreatants.)

Closing Song

10:45 P.M.
Recreation/free time

11:30 P.M.
To sleeping area

12:00 MIDNIGHT
Lights out

SUNDAY

7:15 A.M.
Rising bell

7:45 A.M.
Morning prayer

Opening religious song to set the mood for prayer

Reading: **1 Thessalonians 5:5–11**

Closing: Invite one retreatant to say an original, simple prayer or blessing for the group during this final day of the retreat.

8:00 A.M.
Breakfast

8:45 A.M.
Warm-up exercise: Sing songs as suggested earlier or play "Simon Says," charades, or do an aerobic activity together.

9:00 A.M.
Talk #6—"My Story and the Christian Story" (the talk should be given by an adult team member).

This talk ties the retreat weekend together. The speaker shares personally about his or her own growth as a person, and growth spiritually. Moments in life where the individual has connected to Jesus or received insights from the Spirit can be mentioned—how the meaning of faith has changed for the person through childhood, adolescence, young adulthood and adulthood; who has impacted his or her religious development; how the Eucharist and the gospel nourish him or her; the Christian he or she hopes to become—all these elements can be incorporated into the talk.

9:30 A.M.
"Confirmation" Exercise-small groups

The entire small group focuses on one person at a time, and each of the other members of the group mentions some good quality observed about that person, particularly in the course of this retreat. This is one final opportunity to confirm each other as proclaimers of Jesus' affirmation to each other. It also offers us the encouragement we need to continue to grow as good human beings. (See Exercise #5 sheet at the end of retreat materials.)

10:45 A.M.
Break

11:00 A.M.
Closing service (sit in the prayer circle in the large group around the candle, crucifix, and New Testament)

Leader: Announce that it is time to bring about closure to the weekend. Make any practical remarks, first about departure and then give a brief personal sharing of your feelings about the weekend. Invite anyone who also wishes to do so to share something now.

Distribute letters of confirmation from parents; give a final "greeting of peace" to each other. Sing one of the songs together you have learned during the weekend (standing arm in arm in a large circle). Note: It is important to have a letter for every retreatant. (See sample instructions that follow.)

12:00 P.M.
Lunch, or depart

RETREAT REUNION
If more than a month will elapse between this weekend and the Rite of Enrollment, we suggest that each small group gather some evening for an hour of sharing about how their life has been since the retreat. A few songs and shared prayer should also be part of the reunion.

SAMPLE OF LETTER (from Retreat Director)

Dear Parent or Guardian:

As you know, your son/daughter/foster child/stepchild/grandchild will be attending a weekend retreat as a part of his/her preparation for confirmation. The retreat will be held dates/times_____, transportation information_____, names of adults in attendance on the weekend_____, place_____, emergency phone #_____. No electronic devices are allowed.

I also write to you confidentially to enlist your help. As you know, a synonym for "confirm" is "affirm," in the non-sacramental (yet still, sacred) sense. We would like you to write a letter of "confirmation" which we will give to the retreatants as a surprise at the end of the retreat (i.e., one letter from father, one letter from mother (or foster parent, stepparent, grandparent), if both are living. Tell your teenager, please, how you feel about him/her and the good points you notice in him/her. (Please do not use this letter as a time to offer corrections!) It is vital that everyone on the retreat receive letters which are positive. I am including a sample to help you. (Then tell them where to mail, e-mail, or drop off letter, and the deadline date.)

Thank you for your cooperation. I pray with you that your teenager will grow humanly and spiritually during our three days together.

Sincerely,

(your name)

PENANCE SERVICE

Sponsors and confirmation candidates gather at the parish church.

OPENING HYMN

FIRST READING (READ BY A CANDIDATE)

Psalm 73:21–26

> When my soul was embittered,
>   when I was pricked in heart,
> I was stupid and ignorant;
>   I was like a brute beast toward you.
> Nevertheless I am continually with you;
>   you hold my right hand.
> You guide me with your counsel,
>   and afterward you will receive me with honor.
> Whom have I in heaven but you?
>   And there is nothing on earth that I desire other than you.
> My flesh and my heart may fail,
>   but God is the strength of my heart and my portion forever.

SECOND READING (READ BY A SPONSOR)

Luke 15:1–7

> Now all the tax collectors and sinners were coming near to listen to him. And the Pharisees and the scribes were grumbling and saying, "This fellow welcomes sinners and eats with them." So he told them this parable: "Which one of you, having a hundred sheep and losing one of them, does not leave the ninety-nine in the wilderness and go after the one that is lost until he finds it? When he has found it, he lays it on his shoulders and rejoices. And when he comes home, he calls together his friends and neighbors, saying to them, 'Rejoice with me, for I have found my sheep that was lost.' Just so, I tell you, there will be more joy in heaven over one sinner who repents than over ninety-nine righteous persons who need no repentance."

THIRD READING (READ BY A DEACON OR PRIEST)

Luke 15:11–32

> Then Jesus said, "There was a man who had two sons. The younger of them said to his father, 'Father, give me the share of the property that will belong to me.' So he divided his property between them. A few days later the younger son gathered all he had and traveled to a distant country, and there he squandered his property in dissolute living. When

he had spent everything, a severe famine took place throughout that country, and he began to be in need. So he went and hired himself out to one of the citizens of that country, who sent him to his fields to feed the pigs. He would gladly have filled himself with the pods that the pigs were eating; and no one gave him anything. But when he came to himself he said, 'How many of my father's hired hands have bread enough and to spare, but here I am dying of hunger! I will get up and go to my father, and I will say to him, "Father, I have sinned against heaven and before you; I am no longer worthy to be called your son; treat me like one of your hired hands"' So he set off and went to his father. But while he was still far off, his father saw him and was filled with compassion; he ran and put his arms around him and kissed him. Then the son said to him, 'Father, I have sinned against heaven and before you; I am no longer worthy to be called your son.' But the father said to his slaves, 'Quickly, bring out a robe—the best one—and put it on him; put a ring on his finger and sandals on his feet. And get the fatted calf and kill it, and let us eat and celebrate; for this son of mine was dead and is alive again; he was lost and is found!' And they began to celebrate.

Now his elder son was in the field; and when he came and approached the house, he heard music and dancing. He called one of the slaves and asked what was going on. He replied, 'Your brother has come, and your father has killed the fatted calf, because he has got him back safe and sound.' Then he became angry and refused to go in. His father came out and began to plead with him. But he answered his father, 'Listen! For all these years I have been working like a slave for you, and I have never disobeyed your command; yet you have never given me even a young goat so that I might celebrate with my friends. But when this son of yours came back, who has devoured your property with prostitutes, you killed the fatted calf for him!' Then the father said to him, 'Son, you are always with me, and all that is mine is yours. But we had to celebrate and rejoice, because this brother of yours was dead and has come to life; he was lost and has been found.'"

SUNG (OR RECORDED) MEDITATION SONG

BRIEF HOMILY
By a priest or deacon on the need for forgiveness and the significance of this service, prior to Easter and the celebration of confirmation.

INDIVIDUAL CONFESSIONS
Piano, organ, or guitar music; or recorded hymns; or classical music should be played softly while individuals receive the sacrament of reconciliation. When all are finished, the priest invites the congregation to stand.

Priest:
My brothers and sisters, let us rejoice that our God gives us a sacrament that wipes away sin, softens our hearts, and gives us the grace of a closer union with him and with each other. Let us pray for the needs of all in our community on this special night. (Either a group of candidates can have prepared special intercessions [about six or seven] or the priest can invite spontaneous prayers from all assembled.)

Priest:

Dear Lord, you have heard our needs through these intercessions and those still held in our hearts. Hear us, we beg you, and be gentle with us, for you are our Shepherd and we are your sheep. Amen.

CLOSING HYMN

Procedure of receiving sacrament (review)

1. Examine your conscience—in your mind and heart review your life since your last confession. Is there any serious sin? Are there patterns that have crept into your life which are either sinful or could lead to sinful behavior?

2. Enter the reconciliation room. You may either sit before the priest or kneel behind him.

3. Tell the priest how long it has been since your last confession; then tell him your sins.

4. Recite an act of contrition or sorrow for your sin. (You may use, "O my God, I am heartily sorry for having offended you who are worthy of all my love. I promise with the help of your grace to amend my life. Amen.")

5. Receive the absolution of the priest (he makes the sign of the cross saying your sins are forgiven).

6. After leaving, say the prayers the priest has given you as a penance; if he has given you an action to perform, you will have to wait for the appropriate time.

SESSION 24: Confirmation Rehearsal/"WAITING" PRAYER SERVICE

Suggested Time: 75 minutes

On an evening prior to the celebration of confirmation, we suggest a short rehearsal (approximately 45 minutes) so that sponsors and candidates feel secure about the ceremony. Included in the rehearsal should be a brief education about two important symbols during the ritual of the sacrament:

1. "The laying on of hands"—This is an ancient and common symbol in the Bible by which the grace of God is given through one person to another. At confirmation the bishop and all the priests present extend their hands over the candidates and pray for the gifts of the Spirit.

2. "Anointing with chrism"—Chrism is oil that has been blessed by the bishop. Chrism, a word coming from the same root as "Christ" (God's anointed one), has to do with anointing with oil, an ancient symbol of strength. The anointing in confirmation symbolizes the strengthening in the Spirit we receive in order to be witnesses for Jesus Christ. The bishop makes the sign of the cross with the oil on each candidate's forehead, which is a spiritual "sealing" as a full member of the church. The candidate responds "Amen" to symbolize that he or she does indeed wish to be a full member of the Christian community.

"WAITING" PRAYER SERVICE

We can sometimes get quite wrapped up with the practicalities and arrangements of celebrating sacraments (such as at baptisms, first communions, and weddings). We wish not to lose sight of our spiritual preparation for this sacrament, and we combine our rehearsal with a short prayer service. The theme is "Waiting for the Spirit," as the apostles awaited the Spirit prior to Pentecost. The time frame is 20 to 30 minutes. Seat all candidates and sponsors in a circle of chairs. This may be possible in the sanctuary; if not, perhaps the church hall would suffice. Dim the lights and put several lighted candles in the center of the prayer circle.

OPENING SONG
We suggest repeating in mantra-like fashion a short hymn to the Holy Spirit to help create a mood for prayer (e.g., *Veni Sancte Spiritus,* from the music of Taizé).

Recite together: Psalm 139 (in Journal).

READING
From Acts 2:1–2

Quiet Time: (5 minutes)

Invite Spontaneous Prayer: (5 minutes)

A LITANY OF THE HOLY SPIRIT
The response is: "Come, Holy Spirit."

Leader: Into our world, weary of violence and war
(response)
Into our nation, needy of guidance
(response)
Into our families, longing for healing
(response)
Into our parish, praying for unity
(response)
Into our hearts, seeking your grace
(response)

The response is "Spirit, give us strength."
Leader: To be witnesses of Jesus
(response)
To speak against injustice
(response)
Not to fear the disapproval of others
(response)
To be faithful when it is difficult to do so
(response)
To be prophets for our day
(response)

The response is "Refresh us, Lord."
Leader: With your rejuvenating grace
(response)
With your tenderness and mercy
(response)
With your comfort and guidance
(response)
With your Spirit which ever renews
(response)

CONCLUDING PRAYER

Come, Holy Spirit, and renew the suffering face of this earth. Bless our parish community as we eagerly await your coming again into our midst at the celebration of confirmation. Keep us all free from harm as we expectantly await your outpouring of blessings upon us. Amen.

Suggested closing hymn: "Come, Holy Ghost"

A FINAL COMMENT: MYSTAGOGY

The fourth period of initiation according to the R.C.I.A. is called *mystagogy*—"instruction in the mysteries." Now that the candidates are fully initiated into the sacramental life of the church, they will be instructed in a more specific way about the faith. For these young confirmation candidates, we trust that the whole thrust of this sacramental preparation process has helped them to view this sacrament as a deeper involvement in the Christian community. It is our hope and prayer that, for the newly confirmed, mystagogy will consist of:

1. Regular practice of the sacramental life;

2. Involvement in and service to the Christian community;

3. A keen sense of justice and the willingness to work for it in the world;

4. Ongoing religious education throughout adult life.

As we well know, just as young persons need support during the preparation period for confirmation, they will also need help and parish concern after receiving the sacrament. Very often there is very little in the parish to attract and involve older teenagers/young adults. We tell them that they have now become "adult Christians," and yet we fail to provide them with any real role within the community. One might rightly ask if young confirmed parishioners are given the opportunity to represent the concerns of their peer group on the pastoral council or parish committees. Do they assume significant roles during liturgical celebrations? Are they invited into catechetical or peer ministry work with younger youth in the parish? Are they provided with concrete opportunities in retreat work and ministries of justice, outreach, and service? Are there opportunities also for continuing religious education? It is structured opportunities that we wish to emphasize here—in parish leadership, liturgy, service, and education. As a matter of course, it is our suggestion that the post-confirmation period or year be just as carefully organized by the parish staff or youth ministry committee/team as were the years preceding confirmation. Parishes that do this give real testimony to their concern for young Catholic Christians, and demonstrate a concrete commitment to the life of the future church. Confirmation is thereby removed from the status as a sort of completion or "graduation." These points of view may indicate the necessity within the parish not only to be more sensitive to the needs of emerging young adults, but perhaps also to provide them with staff persons or youth ministers who can devote their energies to this very important ministry. In a reassessment of their priorities with regard to young people, we would hope that increasing numbers of parishes would not neglect the population just beyond the age of confirmation, so that these young Christians are not left bereft and unguided in their struggles to find a meaningful place in the life of the church community.